Eternal Hope

Jim Chatterton

Copyright © 2012 Jim Chatterton

All rights reserved.

ISBN: 1478342234
ISBN-13: 978-1478342236

DEDICATION

I owe a large debt of gratitude to so many wonderful people. Even though I fought some of them all the way, nobody ever gave up on me, and for that I am eternally thankful.

Dr. Schiffer, the Neurologist at UMC hospital that diagnosed my stroke and saved my life. Dr. Roger Wolcott who took over my treatment once I left the acute ward. Without Dr. Wolcott and his amazing staff I honestly don't know where I would be today. He is one of the nicest people you could ever hope to meet, and I have absolute respect and admiration for him.

The doctors, nurses, and all the staff members at UMC who patiently put up with me for so long, took great care of me, and understood my need for independence and self-reliance.

All the staff at the Transitional Learning center in Galveston, Texas. Without these incredible people, I would never have understood the true extent of my injuries, and even though I battled them all the way, I truly believe that my stay at the TLC was fundamental to my subsequent recovery.

Dr. Zgalijardic (or Dr. Z as everyone knew him), saved my sanity, and probably my life when he finally sat down with me and explained exactly what it was I was experiencing. Up until that moment I had genuinely believed that I was going insane.

The incredible rehabilitation staff that worked with me for so long after I returned home, and pushed me to try harder than I ever believed possible.

Dr. Hendershot, and his wonderful staff, especially his nurse Renee. To this day they continue to take great care of me, and on occasions when I have been less than dedicated to keeping up with my medications (especially the blood thinners), they have patiently and firmly reminded me of my responsibilities to myself and my family. I have great respect for Dr. Hendershot and his staff, and I owe them so much more than I can ever repay.

All the many friends that supported me throughout, and continue to do so to this day, and my two children Karen and Philip that stood by me all the way and helped me through the darkest moments of my life. I owe them everything.

Finally, but by no means least, my beautiful wife Glenda, who saw me and accepted me for what I am, not for what I could be.

CONTENTS

	Acknowledgments	i
1	Chapter 1	1
2	Chapter 2	Pg 4
3	Chapter 3	Pg 8
4	Chapter 4	Pg 12
5	Chapter 5	Pg 17
6	Chapter 6	Pg 23
7	Chapter 7	Pg 34
8	Chapter 8	Pg 37
9	Chapter 9	Pg 45
10	Chapter 10	Pg 49
11	Chapter 11	Pg 54
12	Chapter 12	Pg 56
13	Chapter 13	Pg 61
14	Chapter 14	Pg 65
15	Chapter 15	Pg 73
16	Chapter 16	Pg 78
17	Chapter 17	Pg 84
18	Chapter 18	Pg 90
19	Conclusion	Pg 92

JIM CHATTERTON

ACKNOWLEDGMENTS

This book would never have been written without help from my amazing wife, Glenda. Without her ever patient input, I would never have gotten this project off the ground. Along with my children, Karen and Phil, they were always there as I searched for a word, or for a sentence, more often than not at inopportune moments for them.

I can't even begin to tell you all how much I love and appreciate you.

CHAPTER ONE

May 3rd 2007. I remember that day as clearly as I remember Charles and Diana's wedding, and John Lennon's assassination. It was also the last day that I remembered for several months. My name is Jim Chatterton. I was 46 years old, and it was the day I suffered a massive stroke that changed the course of my life forever.

I had been experiencing a series of unusual events in the months building up to this cataclysmic event. I would stumble, slur my words, feel completely disoriented, and have huge gaps where everyday memories should have been. It was like I was drunk.

I never understood what was causing this phenomenon. The only constant in all of it was that my blood pressure was sky high. I scoured medical websites for answers, and made several visits to my doctor. Each episode lasted anywhere from 15 minutes up to 2 hours or more, and they were getting noticeably longer each time I had them. By the time I reached the doctor's office they had subsided, and I found it difficult to explain what had happened.

Like most people, I thought I knew what a stroke was. I also believed – wrongly – that strokes only affected older people. So I discounted this theory right from the very beginning. I had convinced myself that my blood sugar levels were causing these issues, so when the test revealed this wasn't the case, I genuinely had no idea what was going on. I even wondered if it was a psychological issue.

The good news was that I knew my blood sugar levels were good, and that just about everything else in my body was in great shape. I later learned that what I had been experiencing were Transient Ischemic Attacks; otherwise known as TIA's, or mini strokes.

TIA's are known as mini-strokes because they share the same underlying causes of strokes: A lack of blood flow to the brain causes stroke-like symptoms (confusion, slurred speech, weakness on one side of the body etc.) These symptoms are temporary, and usually dissipate within 24 hours. They are seen as a warning sign of a future stroke.

Looking back, it now seems obvious that I was heading for a stroke. I feel foolish for not recognizing the symptoms. My body was trying to tell me but I didn't listen. I paid a heavy price for my intransigence.

I was frightened, an emotional train wreck. I didn't know what was happening to me, and I wasn't in control. I was a spectator to my own downfall. Alone and isolated, I was a prisoner in my self-made mausoleum. My emotions ran the whole spectrum, all seemingly at the same time: Total confusion to abject sorrow. Anger to self-pity - why me? And everything in between.

Until this point in my life, I was Clark Kent: A Superman incapable of being hurt. I was going to live forever. It's amazing how humbling it can be to be proved wrong and to be forced to face your own mortality.

So I ignored it. I put it down to one of those series of unexplained events that we experience now and again in our lives. I thought (hoped) that it would go away on its own, and that my life would return to normal. I was wrong.

My doctor had repeatedly warned me that my blood pressure was too high, especially on the bottom line. Having no medical knowledge, I never understood what the difference was between the top and bottom numbers. I knew that 120/80 was the optimum, but that was as far as my limited understanding went. I suspect it is the same with the vast majority of the world's population.

I was prescribed blood pressure medication, and I took them. When I had them and when I remembered. There is a reason why they call high blood pressure the silent killer: It doesn't hurt. In fact, it feels normal. It creeps up on you unseen and unfelt. Then it strikes.

I know now that a high number on the top indicates the risk of heart attacks and heart related issues. A high number on the bottom indicates a risk of stroke. I also know that it is something that should be taken very seriously and not ignored. To the day I die, ignoring this will be the greatest mistake I ever made. If I can prevent just one person from suffering a stroke or heart attack because of high blood pressure, then this book would have achieved its purpose.

CHAPTER 2

Originally from England, I moved to America in September 1999. I had recently married an American lady by the name of Alison, and we planned to start our new life together in the United States. We married in Scotland, and then I followed her over to America as soon as I could thereafter.

My new wife worked as a nurse in New Mexico. It was only a small town, and it didn't offer any of the opportunities for IT specialists like myself that the bigger cities offered. So we decided to move as soon as I obtained a work permit.

I have always considered myself to be very fortunate in that my two children – Karen and Philip – are not only my children, but also my best friends. They moved to America from England shortly after my own move. My life was complete, and the future was full of promise for all of us.

I had applied for several jobs, but the one with the most potential was the one I was offered at Texas Tech University. The benefits package was excellent, which turned out to be a huge blessing in the years that followed. So we moved to Texas.

Work for me was a happy place; a place I always enjoyed being at. The people I worked with were always friendly, and the atmosphere was jovial and positive. I was a Network Administrator for Texas Tech University, a large university based in Lubbock, Texas, USA.

I had worked hard to get where I was, and I regularly took industry related certification examinations such as Microsoft, Cisco and Novell. My future was full of promise, and I was set for life. Or so I thought.

I had two major passions outside of work. One was the game of darts. Huge in England, it is an underground, but very thriving sport (depending on one's definition of sport) here in the United States. The other was hiking and Backpacking. I love the smell of the forests, and the way that nature reminds us of our own minute insignificance on this beautiful planet we call Earth.

I had always wanted to complete a backpacking trip named the Lost Coast Trail, which is a 25 mile section along the rugged and isolated beach in the Kings Range National Conservation Area in Northern California. It is wild and uncompromising, with the reputation for having one of the wettest coastlines in the United States. Bears, Mountain Lions and snakes roam freely, and there are several long stretches where the beach is impassable at high tide. It is a daunting undertaking, and cannot be approached lightly. It was the thought of attempting this trail that kept me going, even through the darkest moments of my recovery.

I had always loved the game of darts. I had enjoyed some success when I lived in England, and I continued to practice and participate when I moved to America. I had been fortunate enough to have gained somewhat of a reputation for being a good player locally, in Lubbock, and even more fortunate when two businessmen joined forces and offered to sponsor me, affording me the opportunity to travel the vastness of the United States to participate in the large tournaments held throughout the nation on most weekends.

Naturally I accepted the invitation, and so in January 2007 I began to travel America, competing in the American Darts Organization (ADO) sanctioned tournaments. I hadn't played in many tournaments for several years, so I was surprised at the levels of success I managed to achieve. I began in January 2007 in Philadelphia as a complete unknown, and by the end of March I was ranked as high as 14th in the entire nation. I was very pleased with my efforts, as were my sponsors.

At this point in my life, everything was perfect. I had a good career that I thoroughly enjoyed, I thought I had a happy marriage - which turned out to be completely untrue - and my children and grandchildren were close to me and doing very well in their lives. My darts career was looking very promising, and I loved relaxing in the great outdoors whenever I was able. Little did I know that everything was about to change, and that my life was about to be completely ripped apart.

It was around this time that I began experiencing the TIA's. I remember a particularly bad one when I was participating in a regional darts tournament. It was held in San Angelo, Texas, and the winner qualified for the national singles tournament later in the year. This was held sometime around March 2007, and all of the best players from my region were in attendance. I had played well in the first rounds, advancing to the final rounds with relative ease. Then, without warning, it struck. I only know what happened next from what I heard from the other players.

Not only did I lose every game 3-0, it seemed to everyone in attendance that I was completely inebriated. I couldn't speak properly, slurring my words whenever I spoke. I was unsteady on my feet, and I was unable to mark the games that I was required to keep score for. I acted like I didn't know anybody there. The other players were stunned by my appearance as they had never before seen me like that.

I was driving that day, and I was completely sober. All I had drunk was coke and water. This wasn't the first time that this had happened to me, but it was the most severe by far. One of my friends drove me home, and it wasn't until the next morning that I returned to normal.

I have a complete blackout of any memories lasting from early afternoon right through to the next morning – the longest and most frightening of anything I had ever experienced. The next day I felt terribly sick to my stomach, and totally disoriented with both myself and my surroundings. I was shaking and unable to concentrate on anything whatsoever. I knew something needed to be done, as my health was spiraling downwards at an alarming rate.

The TIA's began occurring more frequently, and the effects were lasting increasingly longer each time I had them. I still didn't link my high blood pressure to these incidents, and continued to foolishly ignore it. I went to the doctor's office a few times, but not nearly enough. I still thought I was Clark Kent. Even when I saw the doctor, I didn't explain clearly what was happening, and I was explaining the symptoms that I had self-diagnosed, which had absolutely nothing to do with what I was actually experiencing. So it came as no surprise that he couldn't diagnose my symptoms correctly. I have no one to blame but myself for the way it all turned out, and it is a lesson I will never forget.

CHAPTER 3

And so it continued until May 2nd 2007.

On that day I had a particularly bad TIA. It lasted what seemed like hours, and it left me feeling sick, weak, and disoriented afterwards. They always did. So that day I stayed home.

Immediately upon waking that morning, I knew something was wrong. I felt groggy, unsteady, and confused. I was shaking, and I found it difficult to concentrate on anything at all. I knew I was either in the middle of, or about to have, another episode. I felt terrible, and I knew I would be useless if I went in to work. I also knew that I would be unable to remember anything of what was unfolding, so I stayed in bed.

All I remember was that I felt grumpy and that I needed to be left alone. This was very unlike me. Normally I am a cheerful, happy person, and this was totally out of character for me. I don't remember any specific events from that day; all I know is what my family has told me.

By the end of the day Karen and Phil had become deeply concerned for my health. They had called me sometime during the morning and were surprised by my reaction. I was aggressive towards them, and what I was saying made absolutely no sense whatsoever. Karen's initial thoughts were that I was suffering from a huge hangover, so at first she ignored it, but as the day wore on she realized that it was something much more serious.

Like most people that drink on a regular basis, I suffered from hangovers. I never considered myself an alcoholic, but I did like to drink on most evenings. It is painful for me to admit this, but I have to be brutally honest with myself, otherwise this will not work. I went out most evenings to the bar to play darts and to practice, and although I hardly ever went home rolling drunk, I always drank enough to make sure that I felt it the next morning.

Looking back with hindsight, I have more questions than answers. Why did I do that? Did it cause my stroke? If I had not drank so much could I have prevented my stroke? Was I an alcoholic?

The answers are more painful than the questions. I did it because I was in an unhappy marriage. Both Alison and I knew that, but neither of us cared to admit it at the time. It became a habit that was hard to break. It became my release from reality. I don't think that I was an alcoholic. I still believe that I could have quit at any time and never missed it. As I intimated above, I believe that it was more of an escape from reality, and it became habitual rather than necessary. Either way it was destructive.

I don't think that it necessarily caused my stroke. I wasn't a heavy drinker, just a regular one. I hardly ever drank hard liquor as I have no tolerance for it. I do, however, believe that it contributed heavily to my blood pressure being so high - which I foolishly ignored – which in turn probably caused me to have the stroke. Do I believe that if I hadn't drank so regularly, and taken better care of my blood pressure, that I could have possibly prevented this from happening? Absolutely. Of that I am convinced. I authored my own downfall, and I will regret it forever, and for many reasons.

By foolishly taking the path that I took, I let down not only myself, but more importantly, my family. My marriage may have been unhappy, but I had a great relationship with Karen and Phil. I also had grandchildren to think about. I was selfish, and, to be blunt, a failure as a parent. It is a regret that I will take to my grave, and I try hard every day now to make amends. I owe Karen and Phil so much. They stood by me constantly during the dark days that lay ahead. A father could never ask for more loyal and loving children, and even though I didn't deserve it, it was their strength that pulled me through the most difficult times.

I don't recall if I had been out the previous night. I probably had, so Karen had every right to assume that I had a king sized hangover, although it is embarrassing for me to admit. It was only when it lasted all day and into the evening that both her and Phil started to become concerned.

Karen affectionately calls me her "Favorite Stalker", because she thinks I call her too much. As any parent will testify about their daughter, that definitely isn't the case! That day I didn't call her at all. By early evening Karen had called me several times. Each time I was confused, aggressive, and completely incoherent. All I kept saying was that I needed to be left alone and that I didn't know what was wrong with me. When asked why I needed to be left alone, I responded by saying that I couldn't talk and that I just needed to be alone.

I had stayed in bed all night, all day, and all night again. This is the only time outside of the rare occasions I had been a hospital patient that I had ever done this, and by the time it went dark everyone was concerned about me. Karen and Phil tried to talk me into going to the hospital, but like everything that day, all I was going to do was oppose it. I refused. The conversations became heated, with me as the chief antagonist. All I wanted was to be left alone, so I was.

I have often wondered if I actually had my stroke that day. Looking back, I know I didn't. What I experienced was the most potent TIA I had suffered to date. They were definitely getting worse, and something had to give. The next morning it did, and I will feel the repercussions for the remainder of my life.

CHAPTER 4

The next morning I felt terrible. I was still feeling the after effects of yesterday's mammoth TIA. I wasn't so unsteady on my feet, or shaking, but I did feel disoriented and confused. However, I had missed the previous day of work and I was determined I wasn't going to miss a second day. I still didn't know what was happening, or why. I had never heard of TIA's at this point in my life. I only found out what they were after I suffered the stroke, when the Neurologist told me in hospital.

May 3rd was a Thursday. I remember it well. A little before 8am, I was sat in my office talking to my work colleagues and friends. We were engaged in the kind of small talk experienced in every office all over the world before the work day is about to begin. I remember a growing feeling of anxiety building inside me. Even though we were only discussing the weather and how bad the traffic had been getting into work, I was having great difficulty comprehending what was being said. I couldn't take it in.

It must have been obvious, because my colleagues were looking at me with greater and greater concern. I was feeling foolish and trying to hide my confusion but it clearly wasn't working. I was frustrated at my lack of understanding and coordination. The words

I was hearing from my colleagues seemed to merge into an incomprehensible noise, and I began to lose any sense of where I was or what I was doing.

As the work day began, I hid myself in my office, hoping the heavy clouds would lift from my mind and allow me to function. They didn't. If anything, they got worse, and I found myself drifting in and out of reality and consciousness. My body had been pushed beyond its maximum tolerance, and now it was giving up.

I remember feeling surreal that morning. It was like I knew something major was going on, but I was viewing it from a different vantage point. It was as though I was looking down at myself in the third person, like an interested spectator watching the events as they unfolded. I felt a peacefulness wash over me, calmness the likes of which I had never known. I knew that I was staring directly into the face of my own mortality, and it was the most powerful spiritual feeling I have ever encountered.

My friend and coworker, Brooks, had this to say about the events that followed:

"I received a call from a co-worker (Tony) around 9:00 in the morning saying that he thought Jim may be showing signs of having a stroke. He asked me to go to Jim's office and get my opinion of his condition. I got to his office and he didn't look any different. I wasn't alarmed at first glance because I didn't notice any paralysis of his face or any problems with his speech, which are some of the more common symptoms that a stroke victim will display. The first sign that I saw came when he attempted to call his wife. He paused in the middle of dialing the number and hung the phone up. Then he attempted to write down the phone number and he paused when he got to the number 8. Jim looked up from his pen and said that he couldn't remember how to write an 8. So I wrote it for him and he went to dial the number again and his

brain couldn't even recognize the 8, so he couldn't finish dialing again.

A little while later Jim complained of his left leg hurting and that it felt like it was going numb. Once this happened, I knew something was wrong. I tried to convince him to let me take him to the ER and he was strongly against that. We did settle on him agreeing to let me take him to his PCP, or primary care physician. I remember us talking in the car on the way to his doctor's office about what was happening to him and we both thought it to be less serious than it turned out to be. I think that was a good thing though. If anything, I think it helped calm him down which was good since his blood pressure was so high. Once we got to the doctor's office he thanked me for the ride and insisted that he go in to the office by himself. I asked him if he was sure he didn't need help and he said he was good. I watched him to make sure that he made it into the doctor's office and then I went back to work.

On my way back to work I passed an ambulance. I didn't find out until later that the ambulance I passed was for Jim. Apparently, the doctor's office personnel took one look at him and called the ambulance to come get him and take him to the hospital. "

It was at this point that my memories began to fade. There is an enormous gap lasting for several months where my memories are reminiscent of early childhood – brief, sporadic, and disjointed.

I remember having difficulties using the phone. I remember trying to write the number down, and feeling completely lost and defeated when I couldn't do it. I remember balking at the thought of going to the hospital. For two straight days, people that cared for me had been trying to get me to go to the hospital. I refused every time. Why, I'll never know. I think it is because I was confused and disoriented, and the fact that I was so disagreeable. It didn't matter that the wall was white. If I had been told that it was, indeed, white, then I would have argued that it was black; such was my level of discontent.

I remember my left leg going numb. It felt remarkably familiar, in that I was losing control and was unable to correspond with my body. It was the exact same feelings and sensations that I had been experiencing with my mind and body for the past few months, except this time it was in my leg. I was ostracized from my own body, and even in the state of extreme confusion that I was in, I realized that I was in dire need of medical attention – urgently.

So I agreed to go with Brooks to the doctors' office. I have no idea why I didn't go straight to the hospital; my guess is that it was one final act of defiance, one last attempt to show that I was in charge of my own destiny.

My memories of the doctor's office are very vague. I know what happened from my later conversations with the staff, some of whom I have remained close friends with ever since. I walked in to a fairly busy waiting room and approached the reception desk. The young receptionist asked me how she could help, and I tried to explain how I was feeling. I must have done a decent enough job of it because I was immediately taken to a private room.

Renee is Dr.Hendershot's nurse, and is one of the most wonderful people that you could possibly hope to meet. We remain friends to this day, and she remembers clearly what state I was in when she walked into the room to see me. "It wasn't a pretty sight," was how she described it. I have no doubt that she is correct.

I tried to explain my situation to Renee, and although I am sure that I did a very poor job of it, Renee recognized my symptoms and called Dr. Hendershot's Physician's Assistant, Natalie, into the room. Together, they took one look at me, and within minutes an ambulance was on the way.

I will never be able to repay my debt of gratitude for what Brooks, Renee, and Natalie did for me that day. I am 100% convinced that by their actions my life was saved. Saying thank you seems so insignificant. If it wasn't for them I wouldn't be here writing about it today.

The ambulance arrived; they placed an oxygen mask over my face and took me to the hospital in Lubbock, Texas. From this point, I have no memories whatsoever. I was drifting in and out of consciousness and fighting for my life. The following chapters, through my several month stay in three different hospitals, are as related to me by Karen and Phil. I will state on record, that without them by my side throughout all of what followed, I don't believe that I would have made it. They gave me the courage and conviction to continue, even when it was too difficult and all I wanted to do was give up and die.

CHAPTER 5

Somewhere between walking into the doctors' office and arriving at the hospital, the whole left side of my body stopped responding. I couldn't move either my leg or my arm, and I was in panic mode. I was having problems breathing properly, and my eye sight virtually disintegrated in an instant. Or at least that is how it seemed.

I was stretchered into the emergency room and was set about by a team of medical professionals. My blood pressure was abnormally high, and the general consensus was that I had suffered a stroke. My mind and body was shutting down and I was frantic.

At the time, Alison was working with medically challenged children through a home care company. That morning, along with her patients' foster parents, Alison was already at the hospital with her patient for a scheduled visit. When she got the call that I had been taken there by ambulance, she met me in the emergency room.

For reasons known only to herself, Alison left as soon as Karen arrived. She stated that she was going back to work, and she did. The medical staff had not decided what to do with me, but Alison left for the day. She didn't return until much later, when I had been transferred to a regular ward.

I was sent for the first round of tests, which included an MRI. I have always been slightly claustrophobic, and the thought of going into the MRI machine sent my already panicked mind into overdrive. Poor Karen had to stand at the base of the machine holding my feet while they did it.

After the MRI, I was back in the emergency room with Karen waiting for the next round of tests. Phil had arrived by this time. The doctors came into the room and were asking me simple questions, such as my name, date of birth etc. Karen was visibly upset when I was confused and unable to answer correctly.

What bothered both Karen and Phil the most though, was that I didn't appear to recognize them anymore. I was looking at them as though I didn't know who they were, and when I did try to speak, my words were mumbled and slurred.

I was sent for a C.T scan, a heart scan, and some other tests. By the time I came back to the emergency room several hours had passed, and I was transferred into a regular hospital ward.

MRI scans are not infallible. When the scan is undertaken on a stroke victim, it isn't always possible to detect if the brain has suffered internal bleeding, particularly if the stroke has only very recently occurred. That is what happened in my case.

Emotionally, I was having a very bad day. Ever since I had arrived at the hospital, I had been extremely agitated and panic stricken. I found it difficult to speak, or to understand even the simplest spoken word. For this reason, I still didn't know what had happened to me, and I was confused and frightened.

My left leg and arm had stopped working, my eyesight had

deteriorated to such a degree that I was barely able to see anything, and I was completely disoriented. To compound the situation even further, my wife had apparently deserted me at the time of my greatest need. It was the worst moment of my entire life, and, even though I can barely remember, it is also something that I can never forget.

When evening fell, I was lay paralyzed in a hospital bed on a regular hospital ward. Alison had finally reappeared, and Karen and Phil were ever present. We all could have been forgiven for thinking that the bad news was over, and from that moment forward nothing else would come as a shock to us. Nothing, however, could have been further from the truth. Nobody in the room was prepared for what happened next, and it sent shockwaves that continue to reverberate to this very day.

A doctor walked into the room, and introduced himself. I will not name him at this time, but is a name that none of us will ever forget. The doctor with no name told us that he was going to be my doctor for the duration of my stay in the Hospital. Everybody had expected that he would announce himself as a neurologist, and diagnose my condition as a stroke.

It is impossible to describe the atmosphere in the room when he announced that this particular hospital did not have any neurologists on their staff at that time, and that he was a hospitalist. According to the website medicinenet.com, a hospitalist is "a board-certified internist who has undergone the same training as other internal medicine doctors, including medical school, residency training, and board certification examination. The only difference is that hospitalists have chosen not to practice traditional internal medicine due to personal preferences."

In other words, he was a doctor who "specializes in the care of patients in the hospital", again according to medicinenet.com. This is a far, far cry from being a neurologist. Rather than diagnose me with having a stroke, he proclaimed that because the MRI didn't reveal any bleeding of the brain, I had suffered a hemiplegic migraine.

The symptoms of a hemiplegic migraine are similar to a stroke, but the effects last only a few days. The doctor stated that I would return to normal in a few days, and everything would be okay. He was also extremely proud of the fact that he was able to diagnose a problem with my naval cavities that one of the tests revealed.

When pressed that I needed the services of a certified neurologist, the doctor with no name became angry and dismissed myself and my families concerns. The only concession he was prepared to give was to discharge me in the current state I was in, and refer me as an out-patient to a neurologist. Understandably, this was not received well with my family, and the conversations with this doctor became very heated.

I do not want to go into too much detail regarding the events of the following two days. At that time it was of vital importance that I received the proper medical attention, and any other issues would have to wait until after my recovery.

During the morning of May 4th 2007, my sister-in-law, Debbie arrived. Debbie is a very experienced RN nurse, and has a very forceful personality.

Debbie and the no-named doctor went outside the room to discuss my situation. There had been no change in my condition: I was still paralyzed down my entire left side and I was very confused and disoriented. Nothing had improved. Their raised voices could be heard from inside the room.

Karen and Alison were then asked to go outside, and the conversation became even more vexed. The doctor stood by his original diagnosis, in that I was suffering from a hemiplegic migraine. He also went as far as to accuse me of being a hypochondriac, and that all these symptoms were only in my mind.

The situation was getting out of control, and the only medical care I was receiving was a treatment for migraine headaches. The doctor wouldn't budge in his assessment, and the hospital didn't have any neurologists on their staff. The whole scenario was like a scene from Hollywood and would have been great viewing if it wasn't for the fact that it was so serious.

The next morning, after a family conference, Debbie took charge of the situation and discharged me from the hospital. I honestly don't know what would have become of me if she hadn't intervened, and I owe her a great debt of gratitude.

I was taken by family vehicle to another of Lubbock's other large hospitals, Texas Tech's University Medical Center, or UMC as it is better known. I wish I had gone straight there in the first place. I know for certain that I will never again set foot in the other hospital as a patient.

As part of his discharge notes, the doctor wrote a letter for the UMC doctors. He wrote "The patient clearly requires psychiatric evaluation", as well as a long spiel regarding alcohol abuse and depression being the cause of my psychiatric issues. To say that I dislike this doctor is probably the greatest understatement I have ever made.

The doctor was wrong with his diagnosis. I had suffered a debilitating stroke. I don't know if I would have made a better, more complete recovery if I had received the correct treatment at the very beginning, but his diagnosis and subsequent refusal to budge from his opinions certainly didn't do me any favors.

CHAPTER 6

Once I had been admitted into UMC, I underwent the same tests that I had previously undergone in the other hospital. Where it had taken most of the day at the other hospital, UMC managed to do the exact same tests in a fraction of the time. As I was being transferred into the acute ward, Karen and Phil were pulled aside by the neurologist and told that I had, indeed, suffered a stroke. Even though they were upset by the diagnosis, they weren't surprised. They were relieved to have finally got some answers, which was a complete contrast to what they had experienced at the other, unnamed hospital.

By this time, I had regained a lot of my speech and it wasn't as slurred as it was previously. I was not as confused, and was noticeably more comfortable once I was received into UMC.

I remained in the acute ward for about a week. During that time the chief neurologist came to visit me with a number of medical students. He explained to both me and my family that I had suffered a major stroke, and that I was facing a long, difficult recovery period. I remember this visit, and I remember thinking to myself "Oh, okay. So I have had a stroke. I should be back at work within a couple of weeks". I had no idea then how wrong I was, and just how difficult the road to recovery would be.

My condition had stabilized, and I was doing remarkably well considering the predicament I was facing. I was constantly cheerful and very optimistic for my future. I had been close to death at one stage, so I was ready to fight with everything I had to make sure I made as full a recovery as possible. My family was relieved, and we faced the future together with optimism. Or at least most of us did.

I was transferred to the inpatient rehabilitation unit, where I remained for around two months. It was there that I met Dr. Roger Wolcott. He was in charge of the rehab ward, and is a magnificent doctor and human being. I credit him and his dedicated, amazing staff for much of my success during the recovery phase, and I can't praise them enough.

My memories of the rehabilitation ward are sketchy at best. I remember having to endure twice daily injections in my stomach, once in the morning, and once every evening. These injections were extremely painful and my whole stomach area was one large bruise. I hated them, and constantly begged the nursing staff to forget to give them to me! Of course they didn't, and with good cause: They were blood thinners, and vital for my rehabilitation. I continue to take blood thinners to this day, although thankfully now they are in tablet form!

My days were filled with therapies of many different kinds, and I was kept busy all day every day. My family and friends visited me every evening, and everybody was outwardly optimistic. I was taken to the various therapy units via wheelchair, and many times I would use my right hand to propel myself in-between the different units.

It quickly became evident that my eyesight was going to be a major problem. I constantly ran myself into walls and found turning corners to be particularly hazardous. Anything on my left side was fair game, and I rarely made even the smallest trips without crashing into something.

It was assumed at the time that I was suffering from left sided neglect, which is common in stroke victims. With left sided neglect, the victim's eyesight is intact, but because the stroke affects all of the left side, everything in the left field of vision is neglected.

Depending on the severity of the stroke, it is my belief that left sided neglect can eventually be overcome, or at least be compensated for. This takes a lot of therapy, and 100% effort and commitment from the patient, and is far from easy. Unfortunately for me, it later transpired that I was suffering visual left field cut, not left sided neglect. This meant that I was permanently blind in my left eye.

Until I began the therapy sessions, I had assumed that the extent of my injuries were left sided paralysis, and left sided neglect. It wasn't until after I had left UMC, and transferred to a specialist brain injury unit that I discovered I had permanent blindness, so my focus was solely on recovering from these issues. Then I began speech therapy, and this is where I became unraveled.

My family and the nursing staff had taken wonderful care of me since my admittance, and I had not needed to write or read anything. It was only when I met Tina - a wonderful speech therapist who was very sympathetic to my issues – that I realized I had lost the ability to read and write.

I was completely floored when I discovered that I could no longer comprehend even the simplest of written sentences. It was compounded by the fact that my short term memory recall was badly impaired. I couldn't remember hardly anything, even moments after I had heard it. I thought I was going insane, and I have never felt so frustrated in my entire life.

I was losing my sanity, and I dreaded going to the therapy sessions with Tina. I hated facing the demons in my own mind. I couldn't get my head around the fact that I was having so many problems with words and numbers. I was an avid reader before my stroke, and this hit me the hardest of all my deficiencies.

In my job as a Network administrator, I was working with mathematics on a daily basis, converting decimal into binary and hexadecimal all the time. As a dart player, I was always good at working out the scores I had remaining, and the ways to get them. Reading was one of my favorite ways to relax in the evenings before I fell asleep. And now I couldn't even add 1+1, or read a children's nursery tale. The bottom had fallen out of my world, and I was staring at the abyss.

It was with these thoughts in mind that I went to a typical Friday afternoon therapy session. These were group sessions, where all of the patients joined together in fun activities. There were between 10-20 patients at any one time, most of them stroke victims similar to myself. Some had been there longer than I had, some shorter. The one thing in common was that we had all suffered brain injuries.

Normally on a Friday afternoon, we would play bingo, a simple game that anyone from aged ten to one hundred and beyond can play. Except me. A number would be shouted, and I would have no idea as to its perceived value. I couldn't understand what the number meant, and I couldn't find it on the paper in front of me. Numbers and letters had been reduced to strange, unrecognizable shapes, and I became more and more frustrated.

I had vivid dreams of waking up in a psychiatric ward, a padded cell where I was constantly bombarded with letters and numbers, and then ridiculed and called stupid because I didn't know what they were. When I was awake, these visions stayed with me, and I honestly believed that I was indeed completely stupid.

Tina sat with me during these sessions, and tried to help me. I was so angry and frustrated that I became inconsolable. I just didn't want to sit there and face these issues. I wanted to close my eyes and make them go away. They didn't.

One of my most vivid memories of my time at UMC occurred as I was going through this spiral of self-defeatism. I had just begun to realize the severity of my situation, and I didn't know if I was ever going to be able to live a normal life ever again. Recovering from this was going to be the most difficult challenge I would ever face, and I didn't think I was up to it.

There was a lady patient who had suffered a stroke, and, like me, was having immense problems coming to terms with her deficiencies. Continuously upset, she fought the therapists all the way. She gave up trying to rehabilitate herself, always saying that it was too hard. A short time later she was transferred to a nursing home where she would be taken care of.

This frightened me to my core. Although we had different individual issues, we both faced the same problems in overcoming them. Everybody in the hospital ward did. I had dreams and visions of ending up in a nursing home myself, and I would wake up sweating and crying. It had reached the point where I wanted to die, to close my eyes and make it all go away.

The only thing that carried me forward was the thought of my children and grandchildren, and the look in their eyes when they came to see me. If I couldn't do it for myself, I owed it to them to not give up. I didn't realize it at the time, but it was the event described above that later inspired me to fight harder than I ever thought imaginable, and to make as good a recovery as was humanly possible.

I don't know what happened to the lady, but I hope she rediscovered her inner strength and continued fighting.

I was at an all-time low. I tried to stop going to the therapy with Tina. I felt guilty, because Tina was such a wonderful person, but I couldn't face up to my problems at that time. Naturally, I wasn't allowed to stop, so I sent up a self-defense barrier, a brick wall between myself and my stupidity: I stopped trying.

My other therapies were going well. I was having Occupational Therapy, which primarily worked on my left hand and arm, Physical Therapy, which concentrated on my left leg, and a therapy I forget the name of which worked on problem solving and other brain related tasks.

I didn't fair too well with the problem solving tasks. Even the simplest of jigsaw puzzles that an average five year old would be able to complete were causing me problems. I think a lot of that was because once a piece went out of view of my limited eyesight, I quickly forgot to look for it. This wasn't the whole story though; my capacity for mental reasoning had taken a big hit, and I had problems with even the most menial tasks.

My biggest memory of these sessions was that almost every time I began working on some puzzle, I would almost immediately develop an almighty headache, one that rocked me to my foundations, and throbbed and hurt like none I had ever experienced. Dr. Wolcott assured me that this was normal, and it was a sign that my brain was trying to respond and heal itself. After some powerful medications the headaches went away, and I continued with my feeble attempts of problem solving.

My hand and leg were not responding to anything, and the coordination on my right side was awful. The good thing about the occupational therapy was that my arm was regularly exercised, which prevented subluxation from setting in.

My own definition of subluxation is this: Unlike a hip joint, that holds a leg in place, the shoulder has no such retaining joint. It is held in place by muscles and tendons. Once a person loses the use of an arm, the muscles become weak and relax, allowing the arm to drop downwards, away from the shoulder. This is a very painful condition, hence the reason why occupational therapy is very important.

Physical therapy was the most difficult of all the therapies in terms of physical effort. It involved lying on gymnasium mats in all kinds of positions, and having the therapists work the leg muscles, trying to elicit a response. Unfortunately for me, my leg never did respond. I didn't know if I would ever walk again, and I began to prepare myself for a life confined to a wheelchair.

Looking back, my physical predicament didn't bother me anywhere near as much as my mental one. I was focused almost solely on my reading and writing issues, and all but ignored my arm and leg. I figured I would worry about that later. My brain couldn't cope with everything that was going on. It was already overloaded, so I placed it to the back of my mind, in the "Later" folder. It was probably a good thing at the time, as trying to overcome everything at the same time would have been too much for me, much the same as it is for a lot of stroke survivors.

My world was a paradox. I spent my days stressing about my mental deficiencies. I couldn't understand why I no longer had the ability to read and write, and it drove me crazy. And yet when I went to the sessions with Tina that addressed those very issues, I shut off and wouldn't face them. Tina was a speech therapist, not a neurologist, and she didn't know what was causing it. Nobody did, and my world had ended.

I was always outwardly calm and happy. From the beginning I wanted to present to the world a confident picture – a picture of a man who knew he was going to make a full recovery. I quickly became a favorite patient for the nursing staff as well as the therapy specialists.

Inwardly, however, I was a train wreck. My whole world had collapsed and I couldn't comprehend all that was happening. I was losing my mind – or so I thought – by my sudden inability to read or write. I was experiencing pounding, stomach wrenching headaches whenever I was asked to attempt even the simplest of mental challenges, or when I was interviewed at any length by the medical staff. I had repeated nightmares of the lady that had given up due to the difficulty of recovery, and I was terrified that I would end up the same way. There was only darkness at the end of the tunnel.

I had lost control over every single function of my life. I wasn't even allowed into the bathroom by myself. Until a person has been in that situation, it is difficult to understand how belittling and degrading it is - especially when you can see no way out of it. My confidence was already shattered, and this put the finishing touches to my complete and utter defeat. And yet I did not surrender.

I managed to maintain a semblance of individuality and control by not allowing the nurses to bathe me. I was paralyzed, so obviously I needed assistance with personal hygiene. I would only allow my family to help me into the bathroom, and to help me dry myself. This sounds silly now, but it was the only way I could keep some kind of control over my whole life.

My room was right in front of the nursing station, and they always kept my door open. I could see how busy they were, even during the night when patients constantly pressed their personal alarms for attention. So I decided right from the start that I wasn't going to add to their burden. I never once called them for assistance in any way.

I think this bothered the nurses slightly, and they were always coming checking on me. I had a great relationship with all the nursing staff and I think they enjoyed having me as one of their patients.

I got into serious trouble one night. My door was always kept open, and the light, noise and activity from the nursing station constantly kept me awake. They didn't like to close the doors so they could keep a check on their patient's safety.

One particular night I was having great problems sleeping. I was having my recurring nightmare of the lady, and me ending up in a nursing home. I wanted quietness, and darkness. I could have used my personal alarm to ask the nursing staff to close my door, although they probably would have refused. So I dragged myself out of bed and collapsed heavily onto the floor. I dragged myself to the door, and closed it. I slid along the floor back to my bed, and then realized that I could not get myself back into it.

The nurses probably heard the bang as I fell out of bed, because within a few moments there was a room full of them, all wondering what on earth was going on. They helped me back into bed, ordered me not to try that again, and left without closing the door. I had problems sleeping all night.

The next day, I was visited by the hospital administrators, doctors, nurses, therapy dogs, and family. The common theme was that I was in trouble for pulling such a dangerous and stupid stunt. I had an emergency alarm just for that reason, and I should have used it. Not only was the fall dangerous, but the floors are not hygienic and I could have laid there for hours if they hadn't heard me. Of course I knew they were right, but in some small way I felt as though I had regained a small portion of control, some small piece of individuality that I hadn't had before. I didn't do it again!

Phil and Karen had been at the hospital religiously every night. Alison had been there at some point on most evenings too. It had not been easy for them either. Karen was a full time mother, full time wife, and part time worker at a pet store. Phil worked full time in a retail store and was going to college. He and his girlfriend lived together. Alison worked full time during the day with a beautiful four year old girl who had profound medical issues.

Phil and Karen gave up every spare moment they had available to spend time with me. Karen often brought my grandchildren along with her, which gave me much to look forward to, and made my days so much more endurable. It gave me the will to continue fighting, if only for their sakes.

Karen's husband at the time, Ben, is a wonderful man who took great care of my daughter and grandchildren. He displayed tremendous patience with the situation, and never once complained about the amount of time Karen was spending at the hospital. I owe a big debt of gratitude to Ben for allowing this to happen.

Phil wasn't so lucky. Spending so much time with me cost him his relationship. It was the last thing Phil needed at that time. He and I were very close, and it hit him hard when I was taken ill. He needed his partner to be understanding and supportive. He got neither. It took him a long time to recover his equilibrium, but he never stopped coming to the hospital and supporting me when I needed it the most. I think the thing that upset me the most was seeing the anguish in Karen and Phil's eyes whenever they came to see me. I wanted to reach out and tell them it was going to be alright. I'm sure I did that, but I don't know if they believed me at that time.

CHAPTER 7

Technology had always played a major role in my life, and now it was more important than ever. I felt blessed that I had chosen the career path that I did, and computers and the wonders of the IT world were always at the forefront of my life.

The hospital had allowed me to bring my laptop into my room, and it became a big part of my therapy, especially with Tina. I purchased a text to speech software program, and this allowed me to access and read website content, and to write emails, letters etc.

I began finding ways around my reading and writing deficits by using my laptop, and for the first time in several months, I felt as if I was making progress. I may not have been doing it myself, but I was doing it nonetheless. And it felt good.

During the sessions with Tina, I tried copying letters and words. Numbers and letters had been reduced to strange, alien shapes, and each time I saw them I saw different meanings and symbols within them. None of them meant anything to me anymore; it was like I was staring at Egyptian Hieroglyphics for the first time, and I had no idea what I was looking at.

When I was copying them, it was noticeable that I was copying like a mirror image; they were back to front. I have no idea why I was doing this. It was the way it came out when I was copying. I didn't even know I was doing it back to front until Tina pointed it out to me, and even then it looked right to me.

I would use my PDA to make spoken notes from Tina. She would give me a list of items to remember, and I spoke them into my PDA to remind me of them. These items could be anything, and the purpose was to test my short term memory, and see if I could recall what she had said.

I was failing this badly. My short term memory was terrible, and just about everything she asked me to remember I had forgotten with a few minutes. I even forgot that I had stored them in my PDA, and it was only when she asked me to replay what I had recorded that knew I had even recorded it. I couldn't remember anything.

I couldn't remember the numbers on a clock face. I couldn't remember the numbers on a dartboard that I had stared at so many thousands of times. I couldn't remember my own birthday, or spell my own name. I couldn't remember any of the basics that we learn as a young child, and I cried myself to sleep every night because of it.

Life was an unbearable round of therapy after therapy, each one as seemingly ineffective as the rest. This is in no way any criticism of the staff; they were all extremely professional and awesome to work with. This was an indictment of my own inability to respond to any of the therapies I was undergoing. Nothing seemed to be working, and I was no better off. Neither my leg nor my arm showed the slightest indication that they were ever going to work again. I was bumping into walls and corridors every time I wheeled myself down any hallways, and I couldn't even recognize my own name. I tried hard in every therapy session except Tina's. I was desperate to show some kind of recovery – anything would have done, just something. I was terrified that the staff would give up on me and send me to a nursing home for the rest of my life.

They didn't. Instead, they showed tremendous patience and belief in me. Dr. Wolcott and his staff are some of the kindest, most professional people I have ever met, and they never gave up on me. It was my own lack of confidence and lack of improvement that was driving my thought process. My impatience was limiting my own ability to recover, and I needed to put this right. I just didn't know how. It took me two years of soul searching before I could achieve this.

CHAPTER 8

Texas Tech had been amazing with me. My sick leave had run out some time back, so they placed me into the long term sick pool. This is an area where people donate their own sick time for unfortunates like me. There were several people I know of personally that gave up their accumulated sick time so that I could continue getting paid.

I felt humbled, and I still do that people could be so caring and considerate to someone like me. Although I always tried to be a nice person, I certainly didn't deserve this, and I will never forget what they did. For all the bad things that we see and read about in the news, human beings have the capacity for so much good, and they display it in so many ways all the time. It just doesn't get reported like the bad news does. I will be forever thankful to the people of Texas Tech University for the kindness and generosity they displayed towards me.

Many of my co-workers came to see me during my time at UMC. They would give up their lunchtimes, or their evenings to come to the hospital and visit me. They often brought gifts, such as food items that I was longing for, and I was so grateful to them. Hospital food is never the best, and after two months of it I would have given anything to taste proper food again!

And so it continued. By mid-July I knew I was ready to leave UMC. Medically I was now stable, and even though I had not seen any changes in my disabilities, the staff had seen enough to know that I would benefit from further, more intensive therapy.

Dr. Wolcott introduced me and my family to a gentleman representing the Transitional Learning Center – or TLC as it is widely known. The TLC is a premier brain injury rehabilitation center based in Galveston, Texas. They had world renowned staff members who are specialists in their fields of brain injury.

The gentleman who visited my room interviewed me as to my suitability to become a patient at the facility. He saw me as an ideal candidate, and offered me and my family a place at the unit.

Dr. Wolcott has experienced so much success with his patients at TLC, that he now runs an extension of the unit in Lubbock. Unfortunately for me, back in 2007 this was not the case, and I would have to travel and stay in Galveston.

Alison in particular thought it was a great idea for me to go there. Karen and Phil thought so too, but were not as sure as Alison was. I was completely against the idea. I had been in hospital for several months and was ready to go home. I had thought that I could continue my therapies as an out-patient and I could recover that way. I still wasn't thinking rationally, although I was a lot better than I was when I was first admitted to UMC. The TLC turned out to be one of the best things that ever happened to me.

I wondered why Alison had been so keen on the idea of me going. It didn't take me long to find out the real reason: The week after she took me down to Galveston, she went on vacation for a week to the Caribbean to see her sister married. If I hadn't gone, I would have been home and she would have had to take care of me.

I don't think I would have been so upset with her if she had just told me the truth. I would have understood. Instead, she kept telling me what a great place it was. The reality was that she couldn't care less what it was like down there as long as I was out of the way and she didn't have to take care of me. That was the beginning of the end for my marriage, although I didn't know it at the time. I am sure Alison did though.

Sometime in July 2007 I was discharged from UMC, and had a few days at home before being admitted into the TLC in Galveston for several more months of intense therapy.

I had low expectations of the TLC, and I was dreading going there. I was adamant I didn't want to go, but my family overrode me, especially Alison. I was going whether I liked it or not. The only thing that had carried me through all that time in UMC was the visits I had from friends and family. In Galveston – which is about 600 miles from Lubbock – I had no one. I was going to be alone.

The long car journey down to Galveston was depressing. All I could think about with each passing mile was the ever increasing distance between me and my family. My anxiety levels grew higher and higher, and I found it difficult to think about anything else.

We stayed overnight somewhere just outside Houston, and then ventured into Galveston the next morning, the day I was due to be admitted. We ate a subdued breakfast in one of the coastal restaurants, even though it felt more like a last supper than a warming breakfast, and then found the TLC building.

The TLC itself is a beautiful building. It sits on the site of an old convent in a very beautiful and picturesque part of Galveston, a few blocks away from the sea wall. It is a quiet area, perfect for rehabilitation from major injuries.

To me though, it looked like an impenetrable fortress. Foreboding, with no means of escape, I felt trapped like a prisoner would have felt after King Henry VIII imprisoned them in the Tower Of London. I begged Alison one last time to turn around and take me home while we still had the chance, but of course she wouldn't.

I was seeing things through the eyes of a depressed, very sick man, so it was natural that I would see things differently than everyone else. The TLC would turn out to be my salvation. I just didn't know it at the time.

We quickly found the reception area, and waited for me to be admitted. I was quiet, frightened, and depressed. I would rather have been anywhere on planet earth than where I was, and I found it very difficult to focus on anything other than my blind panic.

Everywhere I looked, people were being escorted around in their wheelchairs by staff members all wearing the same green tee shirts. These people had all suffered brain injuries or strokes, and it was obvious to me straight away that I fitted right in with these people.

There were some people walking around the complex that didn't look like staff members. They looked more like patients, and I was later proved to be correct in my initial assessment. There were people there with varying degrees of brain injuries: Some were able to walk unaided, but most were not. Some people were a lot worse off than I was with their injuries. Others looked like they were in better condition than I was. The one thing we all shared in common was that we had all suffered a life changing, traumatic brain injury, and the TLC was our one great hope.

The admittance process was quick and painless. I was assigned a staff member to escort me around the complex, and was taken to my new home with my meager belongings.

Because the TLC dealt with different levels of brain injuries, the accommodations were set up accordingly. There were two distinct levels of accommodation: The main, upstairs block was for the vast majority of patients and was supervised 24/7. There were several people to a room, and the worst affected patients were kept in this area.

The lower levels comprised apartment type accommodations, and were for the higher level patients who were near to completing their time at the TLC. Most of these patients could walk unaided, and they had a separate kitchen area where they planned and cooked their own dinners. All supervised of course.

The vast majority of patients, regardless of their physical condition, were normally admitted to the heavily supervised, upstairs apartments when they were first admitted. There was no doubt that I was a higher level patient, and didn't need 24 hour care and supervision. I was horrified at the thought of sharing a large room with patients who – through no fault of their own – were incontinent during the night, and had extremely severe brain injuries.

I had come from a private room in the hospital, where I had been allowed my own privacy and as much independence as possible. For the few days I was at home, I had taken my own medications. My family had arranged them for me in color coded dispensers, but I took them without having to be reminded. I tried so hard to be unobtrusive, and not to be a burden. I wanted my life back. Now I was about to have it all taken away again.

Because of my unusual disabilities, the TLC had allowed me to bring my laptop with me so I could communicate with the written word. This was normally against their policy. No electronic equipment was allowed into the building for the patients. They were very strict with what could be kept with you. Nothing of value was allowed, including just about anything electrical. This was because they couldn't guarantee the safety of personal equipment due to the nature of the patients' injuries. I was an exception, and I was very fortunate.

A financial account was set up upon admittance. A sum of around $160 in cash was to be given to the staff for any expenses we may incur – such as day trips etc. – during our stay. We were not allowed any money of our own, which was just as well because virtually all of us wouldn't be able to use it.

My laptop was my savior from the upstairs apartments. Because it had to be kept safe, I was allowed to stay downstairs in the higher level apartments. I had never felt so much relief in my entire life. I knew I couldn't have stayed in those upstairs apartments. I would have refused treatment and demanded that I go home. I would have missed out on some of the world's best brain injury therapy, but I knew that if I had stayed I would have been suicidal to the point that I don't want to think about what might have happened.

Alison had left very soon after we arrived, and I felt alone, abandoned, and completely disconsolate. For some silly reason, some of the more severely injured patients scared me. I had never been in this environment before, and I didn't know how to handle it. I remember thinking to myself "How the mighty has fallen". I had gone from being a respected Network Administrator with managerial responsibilities, a parent and grandparent, and a responsible member of society to this. I have never felt so much self-pity and despondency. I really didn't want to be there.

I met my case manager, Gerry. Gerry is a lovely lady who tries extremely hard to make the patients' stays as comfortable as possible. I was beside myself with grief and anxiety, and I could hardly understand a word she was saying to me.

I was then wheeled to the dining room for lunch.

As the patients arrived one by one, I had a chance to meet them in person. We sat at the dining tables in no particular order, and waited for lunch to be brought to us. I watched, horrified, as severely disabled individuals attempted to eat their lunch. Through absolutely no fault of their own, lunch was a difficult battle for coordination that was beyond many of the patients' capabilities.

Food was dropped over the floor, over the people trying to eat it, and all over the tables. If I was hungry before, I certainly wasn't by this time. I was no better; I only had the use of one hand, and frequently missed my own mouth when trying to feed myself. The staff members tried their best to help, but it is a sight that will be burned deep into my memory forever.

I knew that I needed to be there. I fitted right in with the other disabled patients, yet every fiber of my mind and body screamed at me to leave. I needed solitude, time to clear my head and regroup myself. I needed to be alone.

Nobody was allowed to leave the dining room until everyone had finished eating. Then we were all taken out together. I had tried to leave on my own but was stopped by the staff. I was livid, and felt like I was being treated like a three year old at nursery school. Looking back, it is obvious why we were treated that way. There were too many disabled people together, with too many physical and mental deficiencies to allow us the freedom I desired. I just didn't see it that way at the time.

I was taken to my new room. It was a downstairs apartment that I would be sharing with a fellow stroke survivor named Daniel. I was left there to set up my laptop and wait for the afternoon sessions to begin.

Up to now, I had only met the director of the facility and my case manager, along with the staff member assigned to me that day. I had met most of the other patients in the dining room. I found out later that most of the higher level patients that lived in the downstairs apartments didn't eat in the main dining hall. They used the kitchen next to the apartments that I had seen earlier.

After I had set up my laptop, I made a quick phone call to Karen and Phil on the pay as you go mobile phone Alison had acquired for me. I had begun to find ways around my deficits, and one of them was to use photographs of my contacts. That way I could call people without assistance from others. I don't think cell phones were allowed - especially with the lower level patients that I was currently classed as because they were too easily lost or broken. I had smuggled mine in, and I wasn't letting it go for anything in this world.

I was taken back to meet with Gerry, and she outlined what I was going to be doing during my stay at the TLC. It sounded much the same as the therapies I had received at UMC, but I was wrong. This therapy was on a whole other level.

I was to have occupational therapy, physical therapy, speech therapy, and neuropsychology therapy. I didn't know it at the time, but it was the latter that had the greatest impact on me, and allowed me to come to terms with my injuries. I credit my subsequent recovery to this treatment, and it is to this, and the doctor involved, that I owe my greatest debt.

CHAPTER 9

The first day was spent mainly with getting associated with my new environment, and meeting the therapeutic staff that would aid so much in my recovery. The therapies would begin in earnest the next morning.

That evening I met my new roommate. Daniel looked like he was in his late 30's or early 40's, and had suffered a stroke. That was all I ever knew about him. Most patients had speech problems of some sort, even if it was only a mild slurring, or forgetfulness of words. This was the category that I fell into, and Daniel was the same.

By this time I had met most of the other patients at TLC. I was shocked and dismayed at the young ages of so many of them. The majority were in their early to mid-20's. In fact, at 46, I was one of the oldest people there, which was in stark contrast to my time in UMC when I was probably the youngest patient there.

Motorcycle and car wrecks accounted for the majority of the young patients, and I was saddened to see so many young adults suffering in this way. Some would recover to lead normal, healthy lives. Others would never be that lucky. It put my own predicament into its proper perspective, and I realized that as sad as it was, I had at least enjoyed my life. I had two wonderful children, and – at that time – two very special grandchildren. Some of these young people would never be able to experience these special events and my eyes still well up whenever I think of it.

Daniel and I got along pretty well. We were in similar situations, and were trying to make the most of our recoveries. I had set my laptop up with the Vonage internet VOIP (voice over IP) telephone system. Using this method, I was able to call not only my family in America, but also my sister and brother in England. They had been shocked and stunned when I had my stroke, and were concerned about my recovery. This way I could speak to them myself and hopefully put their minds at ease.

I began my therapies the next morning. I realized very quickly that I had two totally distinct and contradictory sides to my opinions of the TLC. I absolutely hated the rigid, tightly controlled living environment where all my freedoms had been removed, but I loved the therapies and the treatment I was receiving. I knew they were world class, and that my best chance of making any kind of recovery was there. During business hours I enjoyed being there. Outside of those hours I hated every second of it.

It wasn't that I didn't realize why it was so tightly controlled; it was that I wished they would see that I didn't need constant supervision in *every single area of my life.* It was only my second day, and I had already battled with them over the use of the shower. They wouldn't allow me to shower without assistance; I wouldn't allow anyone in the shower room with me. I told them that if this was to be the rules, then I would stay dirty and refuse to shower until they allowed me to do it on my own. I must have been a terrible patient, but the way I saw it, I was fighting for the only thing I had left in the whole world. And that was my independence.

I think I got lucky here. The Occupational Therapist I was assigned to seemed to be in charge of my personal hygiene. The very next morning he upped and left his position. He had been very insistent that I was not able to shower by myself. After he left, I went about my business as quietly as possible, and it seemed to work. Never again during my stay did I get any grief from the staff about this. My biggest issue had been averted.

The routine was fairly simple, and I quickly settled into it. Physical therapy was in the gymnasium and was especially difficult, at least physically. The new therapy that I was introduced to was Neuropsychological Therapy, or Neuropsych for short. This was led by Dr. Dennis Zgalijardic, who I only knew as Dr. Z. It was this therapy that finally answered all my questions and allowed me come to terms with what I was facing.

I had told Daniel that he could use my system to call his wife and children, and he happily accepted. A few days later I regretted making that decision. My already suicidal mind sunk to even lower levels, and I found myself staring into the mirror, telling myself that I didn't want this anymore. I had no more fight to give. I had given up.

I went back to the room after therapy to call Karen and Phil in Lubbock. My laptop was lying on the floor, and it didn't look too healthy. I picked it up, and sure enough the PCMCIA slot where I kept the wireless network card (this laptop was pretty old and didn't have built in wireless capabilities) was cracked and broken. I was unable to connect to the TLC wireless network, and hence I was unable to call Phil and Karen. I still had my cell phone of course, but this was a prepaid phone and I didn't have many minutes available.

I was absolutely livid. I relied very heavily on my laptop for so many things, and I felt helpless and alone. I have never felt as low and defeated in my entire life as I did at that moment. I broke down and sobbed uncontrollably for what seemed like an eternity. Suicide seemed a better option than ever, and I fought all the dark thoughts swirling around in my mind. Eventually I pulled myself together, and in a rage I set off to find Daniel.

I found him in a different part of the TLC. He looked sheepish and guilty. Surprisingly, I stayed very calm when I asked him what had happened. I had envisioned an ugly confrontation, but it was nothing of the sort. Daniel had caught one of my power cords with his wheelchair, which pulled the laptop off the desk as he went by. It was a complete accident, and he felt terrible. He had panicked when he heard it fall, and had galloped away from the scene. All that was left for me was to try to fix it up as best I could.

A staff member took me to the local Wal-Mart where I was able to purchase a USB wireless network device. I had to use the money that was placed in my initial account setup, but at least I was able to get it. Although the connection was weak, I had network connectivity. I guarded the laptop with my life after this.

Later that day I was moved to a different apartment room. Karen had called the head of the TLC and protested vociferously in my favor, and it caused quite a stir. Emotions were running high, not least of which were mine. My moods reflected my pessimistic outlook, and all I wanted was to go home.

My new roommate was a young man named George. He is a lovely young man and we quickly became friends. I felt comfortable with George as a roommate, and the incident with Daniel was quickly forgotten.

CHAPTER 10

Ever since I first started having the TIA's, my confidence, my health, my emotional distress, and my depression kept dropping lower and lower. Every time I thought I had hit rock bottom I found that it was just a glass ceiling leading to another, deeper level. Each time I sank further into the abyss the light at the top looked more and more out of reach. When the stroke hit me I thought I had hit absolute rock bottom. When I found I was paralyzed on my left side I sank even further. When I realized that my eyesight had disintegrated virtually overnight I sank deeper still. When I discovered that I could no longer read or write I thought I was going insane, and I crashed through several basements.

When I began rehabilitation I quickly found out how difficult and painful it was going to be to recover even the most basic of the functions that we all take so much for granted when we are fit and able. This sent me to new levels of darkness and depression, and when I was sent to Galveston, away from the only thing that had given me hope – my children and grandchildren – I thought that it couldn't possibly get any worse.

As I stated earlier, the therapy at TLC was world class, but the living conditions were (by necessity, although I never saw it at the time) a living nightmare for me. With the incident with Daniel, I was ready to give up and join the lady in the nursing home. This life had become too difficult to face, and I was a defeated, broken man.

I didn't know it at the time, but I had finally reached the bottom. This was my basement and I couldn't go any lower. These were the worst moments of my entire life, and although they are painful ones, they are ones I will always remember. Whenever life gets tough now, I think back to that time. It puts anything I may be currently experiencing into perspective, and I realize that things are not as bad as I thought they were.

I kept my demeanor to the staff and the outside world (the staff and other patients were my ONLY world at this time apart from the calls to my family) as friendly and outgoing as possible. I didn't want anyone looking inside me and seeing what I really felt like. If I was giving up, I was giving up on my terms. I had control over absolutely nothing, and in some distorted way it gave me a sense of power that at least I was in control of my own final destiny.

So I drifted in and out of the therapy sessions. Some I enjoyed others I found difficult. I never stopped hoping for some miracle to occur, no matter how small. Perhaps a tiny movement in my finger or toes, or the slightest improvement in my eyesight. Anything would have sufficed. But nothing came, and I had no reason to expect differently.

My situation was about to change however, and the name of that change was Dr. Z. What I learned through Dennis changed my whole outlook, altered my demeanor, and gave me the impetus to begin the monumental fight back to a semblance of normal life.

The first few days I spent with Dr. Z was a continuous

neuropsychological examination. This lasted all day for several days, and like before when I was in the UMC, it caused me to experience massive headaches on a regular basis. Each separate part of the examination seemed totally unrelated to my confused mindset, and I had no idea what exactly I was being evaluated for. My memories are fragmented of this whole experience, and I can only remember small parts of the evaluation process.

A couple of questions he asked me stand out in my memory. One time he asked me if I could differentiate between my left and my right hands. I looked at him like he was crazy. Of course I knew my left and right hands. Why wouldn't I? I was 46, not 2. So he asked me to show him. I looked down at my hands and to my absolute horror I realized that I didn't know which was which! I sat and thought about it for ages and in the end had to make a wild guess.

At this point I accepted that the stroke had made me officially insane and that I would never see normal life again. Of course I was wrong, but it is easy to see with hindsight why I would think that way. Dr. Z assured me that everything was okay and that he would explain everything once he had finished his evaluations in a few days.

I was confused and annoyed. What was happening to me? It got even more confusing the next day when he asked me if I knew what each of my fingers were called. These were just stupid questions to me at the time, and I didn't understand why he was asking me such random rubbish. What have my fingers got to do with knowing the difference between right and left? What was he going to ask me next?

Of course I knew what my fingers were. I had owned them for 46 years and known what they were for at least 44 of those years! And yet when I looked down to show him, I had a feeling of dread that all was not as it seemed. I stared at my fingers for ages trying to prove both Dr. Z and myself wrong. I failed. I had no clue what the connection was, but I was about to find out.

I already knew that I could no longer read or write. I also knew that I had lost all of my math skills. Even the simplest equations were beyond me. These issues were much more profound to me than learning that I couldn't tell my left from my right, or that I didn't know my pinky from my ring finger. And yet together they tell a story. Or at least they do to trained professionals who know what they are looking for.

A few days later, Dr. Z had me in his office. He had gone over the results several times with his staff, and the diagnosis was clear. Up until this point I had thought the stroke had somehow made me partially insane and I had dreams and visions of living in an asylum in a padded cell. These were very real dreams and visions, and they terrified me, but I had no other way to explain why I had lost so many of my most valuable functions.

Dennis sat down across his desk and began to explain my symptoms and what they meant to both him and me. He asked if I had ever heard of Gerstmanns Syndrome. In the same lighthearted manner that I had adopted the whole time I was hospitalized, I responded that I thought he was a music composer. Of course, I was referring to Gershwin, and I knew that when I said it. I had never heard the word Gerstmann. I knew it sounded German, and I was proved correct in that, but otherwise, as usual, I had no clue what he was talking about.

Dr. Z then began to explain what Gerstmanns Syndrome was, and how it affected the people who had it. He explained that Gerstmanns occurs as a result of a stroke or brain injury, and that I was now suffering from it. Finally I had a name for my insanity, and for the first time since all this started, I felt a small ray of hope penetrate the dark clouds within me. Finally I had answers.

Gerstmanns Syndrome has four distinct symptoms which are:

Writing disability

Unable to perform basic math functions

Unable to differentiate between left and right

Unable to recognize the names of the fingers on the hand

In addition to the above, it is common for sufferers to experience aphasia, which is explained as having difficulty with speech, understanding speech, and the inability to read AND write.

There is no known cure for Gerstmanns Syndrome.

Although I had regained my speech, and I was able to communicate effectively verbally, I had lost a lot of my self-perceived intellect when it came to sentence structure and grammatical values. I had difficulty choosing the right words, and I was very embarrassed by it. I definitely had lost the ability to both read and write, so aphasia was a big issue for me.

Every one of the symptoms of Gerstmanns Syndrome struck some huge chord within me. Each one was obvious once it was recognized and pointed out. Each one had different levels of meaning to me, some more hurtful than others. Even though there was no cure, it made me feel so much better just knowing that I had a name for it. I wasn't going insane! Finally I had hope, even though I had no idea how much, if any, recovery I would ever make from it.

CHAPTER 11

This was beginning of a new chapter for me. I was able to come to terms with my disabilities and see them for what they were. I was able to forgive myself for having the stroke, and I was at peace with myself with the repercussions from it.

A huge cloud lifted from my mind, and I began to dare to hope again. I began to dream of making a good enough recovery to be able to experience the Lost Coast Trail in northern California, although at that time anyone would have thought me mad to be even considering it.

I realized that I would never be able to recover until I forgave myself, and accepted the disabilities for what they were. I had to channel all my energy and effort into the recovery phase, and not waste it on self-pity, guilt, anger, and morbid depression. I realized that although I had the best professional help available, ultimately the healing would have come from within.

Although I was a long way from recovery, this was the single most profound day of self-discovery I have ever had in my life. It was a spiritual experience that I doubt many of us ever get to experience, and it is one that I will remember for the remainder of my days.

I began looking at myself in a totally different light. When I looked in a mirror I saw what I hadn't lost, not what I had lost. I became thankful for what I still had to offer, not for what I couldn't offer any more. I became positive and stopped complaining. There were so many more patients that were in a much worse position that I was ever in, and I realized that I had far less to complain about than they did.

All this came about from two little words: Gerstmanns Syndrome. Two words that I had never heard before, but to which I now clung to like I would a piece of driftwood in the vastness of the oceans. The whole focus of my life changed forever, and I vowed never to be negative ever again about any aspect of my life. I was going to fight and fight, and if I failed then it would not be due to lack of effort or commitment.

CHAPTER 12

I had been using text to speech programs on my laptop for some time for communication purposes. I was able to construct emails, read emails, web sites, and just about everything I desired electronically. It seemed only a small adjustment to move completely to the electronic world rather than the paper one. It was a small price to pay. It seemed with my new found outlook that anything was possible with just a little imagination and an "outside the box" approach to my issues.

I began to look at every issue I had as an opportunity to find a way around it. I took it upon myself to find answers to the issues I had. The staff members were impressed with my ability to find ingenious methods, and this encouraged me even more.

I began using colors to help me sort things into order. When cooking, I would color code an excel spreadsheet to coincide with the amount I needed. For example, if I needed two cups of one item I would add one cup (color coded with the set of kitchenware), and then fill cell one with some character to show that I had added one cup. I would repeat this until I reached the row of cells colored red, which meant I had added the desired amount.

I needed help in setting this up at first, but as I became more proficient I used a combination of colors and speech software to attempt it myself. Independence was always foremost in my mind, and I was determined to do things myself. I made lots of mistakes – I still do – but that was never the issue. I was functioning independently, and I loved it.

For oven temperatures I would color code the stove. For 350, I would add a red dot. This would coincide with an entry into a word document that read "Red dot equals 350". This may all seem like a lot of effort to achieve minimal results, and for the average person it is, but for me it meant everything. It gave me the confidence to continue trying new things, and it gave me the confidence and strength of character to face my disabilities head on.

My phone was set up simply. I used pictures of my contacts to call them. If I wanted to add a new number, I would have them call my phone (I had my number written down for me to show them). Then I would add a photograph and add them to my contacts. I felt pretty proud of myself.

I began taking much more notice of my surroundings. By this time, I had been diagnosed with permanent blindness, not left sided neglect. My left eye was completely blind, and the left side of my right eye was blind too. Where before it broke me into little pieces every time I thought about it, now I thought 'I still have the use of half of my right eye. I can see, and I can get around. That is all I need'. It is amazing how a slight change in perception can alter the course of a whole life.

I slowed down in my wheelchair and started turning my head more. I stopped banging into walls and objects. Not all the time, but enough for me to notice a vast improvement. I was making progress.

There still was no sign of recovery in my limbs. I had developed subluxation in my left shoulder, and it was very painful. I began wearing a sling to keep it from dropping further. My hip flexor muscle was all but dead, and my leg was a dead weight. So I kept exercising using the recumbent bicycle in the gym. My right leg was doing all the work, but my left leg was going along for the ride, and it kept the muscles working and active.

I kept working harder and harder trying to see even the slightest signs of recovery. I had a full sized leg brace made for me, and that, with the help of a walking frame and a member of staff moving my leg for me, allowed me to stand up and at least show a semblance of walking. It wasn't pretty, but to me it was like I was a bird being set free from captivity. I had to relearn all the things I learnt as a small child, but this time I knew what I was missing. Every time I felt frustrated or down – which was very often – I quickly reminded myself of those dark days before my diagnosis and the promises I made to myself after I found out. "Gerstmanns Syndrome" became my acronym for life, and I dedicated the rest of my life to getting past it.

I continued in this vein for some considerable time. I worked hard in every area, and I became friends with Dr. Z and his staff. His diagnosis above all others had given me the answers I was seeking, and used it to drive me forward for the rest of my days.

I researched Gerstmanns Syndrome until I knew as much about it as I possibly could. Although it will remain with me for life, I determined I would never use it as an excuse or hide behind it. I would always face it head on.

I had reached a plateau, and it was finally time for me to return home. I spoke with the staff, and they agreed to allow me to graduate from the Transitional Learning Center. They had wanted me to stay longer, but I was adamant I wanted to move on with my life.

In August 2007, Alison and Phil travelled down to Galveston to witness the graduation and to take me home. There was an emotional moment when I said my goodbyes to my roommate George. We had become close friends during our time together. George is a young man who has suffered a great deal, and I greatly admired his inner strength and fortitude. We promised to stay in touch, and indeed we still do to this very day.

My main goal when they came down was to surprise them in the gymnasium. I still had one session of physical therapy to complete before graduation, and I had worked so hard trying to reach the point where my hip flexor muscle would work just enough to allow me to walk to them with the aid of my leg brace and walker. Unfortunately, as much as I tried, it wasn't possible. My leg just wouldn't work. But I didn't give up.

Alicia, my physical terrorist as I called her, helped me to stand up, and pushed my leg forward slowly for me. Together, we walked the 30 feet or so to Phil and Alison. It was one of the most emotional moments of my life, and although I didn't achieve my goal of walking unaided, I did walk to them. Phil welled up with tears, and I think Alison was touched too although she didn't show it.

The graduation was videotaped, and I received a graduation diploma. I made a short speech to everyone present. I had printed it out and given it to Gerry so she could help me. Once it was off the computer I could not read it, and my short term memory was still badly impaired. I forgot most of what I was trying to say, but I bumbled through it with Gerry's assistance.

I had given many speeches and talks in my time in the IT world, and none of it ever bothered me. Yet when I was delivering my final speech I broke down several times. So many thoughts raced through my mind, creating the perfect storm of emotions all at the same time:

A gentleman who traveled down from Lubbock to Galveston at the same time I did came clearly into my mind. He only lasted a short time in the TLC, and was then taken back to hospital. I know he didn't make it.

A lady who was the victim of violent crime was in the audience. This wonderful lady would never again be able to hold her grandchild, or be able to express her emotions as she used to.

The family of a young man who had a motorcycle accident who moved to Galveston to be with him. He will never recover.

A beautiful young girl who was in a motor vehicle accident. This young lady was vibrant and an inspiration to all of us, and yet her body was broken and her mind damaged forever.

The lady back in UMC that had given up and was removed to a nursing home.

And many, many more people that I had met and gotten to know during my time in hospital. Each and every one of us has a story to tell, each with its own unique heart wrenching storyline, and each with its own unique, not yet established conclusions.

All this became too much, and I broke down yet again and just sobbed. The emotion in the room was raw and exposed, and it drove home to me yet again just how difficult it is for all of us to accept these life destroying brain injuries, and yet the vast majority of the people in that room were cheerful and positive, and didn't complain when the going got tough. It made me feel insignificant and it was the most humbling experience I have ever experienced.

CHAPTER 13

I had been in Galveston for around two months. Combined with the time I spent in hospital in UMC, I had been an inpatient at medical facilities for almost five months, and I was ready to get out. I really enjoyed the journey home, especially as we stopped overnight in Houston to visit NASA. They were wheelchair friendly, and we had a great time. One of the 1960's Apollo spacecraft that never launched was in a hangar. It was one of the biggest man-made structures I have ever seen, and it was awe inspiring.

When I got home, I learned that many of my friends had arranged several fund raisers for me and my family during my absence. I had people I didn't even know coming up to me and wishing me well. I felt humbled yet again.

I began outpatient therapy almost immediately, and I quickly got into the routine again. Dr. Wolcott took over my treatment, and I trust him completely. I owe him my life, and he will have my respect and admiration for the remainder of it. By now I knew exactly what to expect and what to do. I had experienced more therapy than I could stand, and nothing seemed to be working. I kept trying as hard as possible though. I had made a vow to myself never to give up, and I reminded myself of it at every opportunity.

I had printed out some photographs of the Lost Coast Trail, and I consumed myself with one day fulfilling my goal of backpacking this beautiful trail. At this point, I am sure that everyone was just humoring me with it. If it made him feel better, then just go along with him. But I was deadly serious. I didn't know when, but I knew I would eventually do it. It spurred me on during the difficult times when it seemed like I was never going to get even the slightest recovery, and all seemed lost, which was most of the time. It was like I had to achieve something that was –at that time – impossible for me to achieve. I had to accomplish something that was greater than the sum of myself, and it gave me something to live for.

For months I went to therapy. Every day I went, both morning and afternoon. I dropped the speech therapy on the recommendation of Dr. Z. All it was doing was frustrating me and showing me what I couldn't do. Nothing positive was coming out of it at all. I was reading and writing just fine with the aid of my laptop. I had that down to a fine art. My attention was now turned solely to regaining my physical prowess, or at least to some manageable degree.

After around a year of therapy, I still wasn't getting anywhere. My hand and arm wasn't doing anything, although the therapists had worked it so much the subluxation issues were subsiding. My shoulder was still painful, but it was a lot better than it was in the TLC. Finally, one day when I was working on my leg, I was pushing with all my worth onto a weightless leg press when I moved it. Only about an eighth of an inch, but I moved it! I cried and cried. Finally, after all this time, I had movement in my leg. It felt like I had won the lottery.

One issue that I had suffered with ever since I began therapy way back in the UMC was my balance. When they stood me up, they asked me to stand up straight. I was wearing my leg brace, and I was using my walker. I stood up to full height and stood straight and proud. Until they put a full sized mirror in front of me. Then I looked like Quasimodo with a slipped disc. I was bending so far over to my right side it looked like I was getting ready to get into the blocks for a 100 meter sprint race.

I had massive problems with my balance. The reason was because I was compensating for my stronger right side and my weaker left side. Because of the brain injury, my mind positioned my body's center of gravity over my stronger side, thus causing the leaning tower of Pisa look. If I straightened myself out properly (according to the mirror, not how it felt to me), then I felt completely off balance and unsafe on my feet. I never learned to completely correct this issue. I still lean over to the right side, although nowhere near as much as I used to do. It is one of the many things that will be with me for the rest of my life, and I just accept it as normal now.

After about another month, I still wasn't making much progress with my leg. I was getting so frustrated with myself, and I found it hard to stick with my plan of never allowing frustration to affect me ever again.

The therapists all had my best interests at heart. And that included my safety. I wanted to push on without using the safety props like my leg brace because I was frustrated with the lack of progress. I was impatient for more, and I realized that I had come to the end of a long road as far as therapy was concerned. I could have continued, the therapists all wanted me to, but I had learned so much in the last year or so and I didn't know how much more we could achieve together.

I thought of the other people that were probably waiting to begin therapy and who probably needed it much more than I did at this time. So I made the decision to go it alone. Right or wrong, I was now on my own and I was more determined than ever to recover enough to hike the Lost Coast Trail. It became my obsession.

The one thing I had constantly avoided (and still do), was to face my deficiencies in public. I felt so embarrassed when people who didn't know me found out that I couldn't read or write, or tell the time, or spell my name, or any of the other countless things that were beyond me. I knew it was silly and that it wasn't my fault, but I felt stupid and pathetic when confronted with these issues. I still do. I hid behind Karen, Phil, or anyone that could shield me. It may not be the correct way, but I will wager that anyone else who has ever been in a similar position knows exactly how I feel when this happens. Even though people rarely say anything, it is written all over their faces. And it hurts.

Chapter 14

Every day I began working on my own. I forced myself to stand up and move along the side of the couch, or in the kitchen using the counter tops. I fell more times than I care to remember and I hurt myself on many occasions, but I was making progress. The therapists would have thrown a fit if they had seen me falling over all the time, but for me the bruises and cuts were all worth it. They showed that I was alive and that I was still able to feel like everyone else.

I used my leg brace and my walker to steady myself, and through sheer will power alone, I made my leg move. Little by little, slowly but surely, my leg started to work. It was very weak and would not hold me without support, but it was moving. At least horizontally. For the life of me I could not get my leg to move up and down, like I would have to if I was climbing stairs. But it was moving.

If I crossed the road to Karen's house (she lived across the street from me), I had to use my wheelchair. I was still unable to walk unaided or move my leg any distance, but around the house I was able to move around the couch or around the kitchen, albeit with a lot of physical effort for not much return.

As the weeks went by I grew stronger, and eventually I was able to hold my weight on my leg as long as my knee wasn't bent. I was able to walk further and further without falling and hurting myself. I was on top of the world. Unfortunately, I was still struggling with lifting my leg, or putting weight on it with my knee bent. If I walked over any kind of rough terrain, I would promptly fall over it as I was unable to get my foot over or around it.

My arm had begun to show signs of life too. I could now move it around and grasp cups, knives and forks. I didn't have much dexterity, and I certainly could not lift my arm above shoulder height. It was very weak; I could barely open a door with it. But it worked.

I left the walker behind and started using a cane. Then I left the leg brace off completely, and just used the cane. If I had to bend over and pick something up I would always fall over, so I obtained a telescopic device that fit in my pocket but expanded to pick things off the floor. This saved me from many bruises and scrapes.

Eventually I left the cane behind too. I had a noticeable limp that got worse the more tired I became, but I was walking on my own! I was so proud of myself. I know it doesn't sound like much now, but just being able to stand up and walk to the door or the refrigerator was a great achievement and it meant the world to me.

I continued to improve. For each two steps forward I would experience five sideways steps and one backwards step, but I persevered and got stronger and stronger until I finally believed I was ready to achieve my biggest goal, the one that had kept me going through all of my darkest days.

By now it was the end of summer 2008. Outside of my family, the one thing that had motivated me the most to recover and never give up was the thought of hiking the Lost Coast Trail. Even though I knew it was too soon, I pressed my brother-in-law - Cesar - to begin planning the Lost Coast Trail. I had worked hard for over a year to get this far, and I wasn't allowing anything to get in my way. We made plans, and set a date. I had already created a website describing my stroke and my subsequent fight for recovery, and now I added some pages outlining our upcoming adventure. I did the only thing that I still felt I was able to do with any hint of accomplishment – I researched and researched everything I could in readiness for our big hike. To say I was excited and motivated is a huge understatement.

I asked Alison if she would take me to the nearest mountains to try out my gear and to see how I would cope with the uneven landscapes that I would be walking on. So she took me to Ruidoso, NM, which is about 250 miles from Lubbock. The area I was going to was very familiar to me, in the Lincoln National Forest. I camped and hiked there a lot pre stroke. It is a beautiful forest, right around the area where Billy The Kid used to roam during the height of the Lincoln Wars.

It was sometime around September 2008, and I was walking – somewhat – without any exterior aids. Alison dropped me off and went to stay in Ruidoso with her sister in a log cabin. At my own request, I was left to fend for myself in the mountains. I didn't know how far I could get, but I planned to attempt the Argentina Canyon trail, which is about six miles and includes plenty of strenuous hiking and lots of uneven terrain. I figured if I couldn't manage this then I was not even close to ready for the Lost Coast Trail.

As soon as she dropped me off it started to rain. Hard. I walked about 50 yards from the trail head when I hit my first bump in the terrain. I fell flat on my face in the mud. I got up and negotiated that hurdle, but in the next 50 yards I must have fallen over 100 times. It was clear that I wasn't ready for this. Nowhere near.

I cursed myself all over the place for being so stupid. How had I got myself into this situation? Through my own stupidity, that's how. I had no cell phone signal and no way to extricate myself. I knew it was folly to try going any further. I was going to end up seriously hurting myself and getting stuck somewhere. I had to stay put at the trail head where I was dropped off.

The rain came down hard. I managed to put up my small one man tent, and I clambered inside. Because I had no strength in my left hand, I wasn't able to properly stake the tent out. The guy lines were loose and the tent was not taut which it needed to be to be totally waterproof. As I was using a single skin tent made out of silicone impregnated nylon – or silnylon as it widely known, I was going to get wet. From both the elements and from condensation.

I stayed there in the pouring rain for two nights and most of the third day. My sleeping bag had gotten soaked through and lost most of its loft. My clothes were drenched and I very cold. Alison was supposed to have picked me up at 10am (I had no alarm and could not read any watch, but I was up early to be ready for her when she came). She never showed up until late afternoon, having decided to spend more time in Ruidoso even though it was pouring with rain. So I just got wetter as I waited.

There was no way to hide the fact that this whole adventure had been nothing less than a complete disaster. And yet I had enjoyed every second of it. Well, all of it except the long wait sat in the rain for the ride home. I was not able to walk over uneven terrain without falling over, and my arm wasn't strong enough to tighten the tent down firmly enough. At this point I should have cancelled the upcoming trip and got stronger. Any sane man would have, but I guess I wasn't sane. All it did was to strengthen my resolve to get stronger and complete what I had started. Nothing was going to stop me from going on this adventure, and nothing was going to stop me from completing it. Madness, I know.

I had less than a month to prepare for the biggest test of my life. I had dreamt of this upcoming moment for a year and a half. When I was lying completely paralyzed on one whole side of my body in a hospital bed, I promised myself that as soon as I was able to walk I was attempting this hike, and nothing was going to stop me.

I originally planned to undertake this hike at the end of 2007. This shows how delusional I was when I planned it. At the end of 2007 I was still wheelchair bound and unable to move hardly anything at all. So I was a year late, but I didn't care. I worked on my treadmill all the hours I could. I walked all over the local neighborhood and around the local park. One thing I did was to purchase two telescopic hiking poles that really helped my balance and kept me on my feet. They also helped me over rough ground and stopped me from falling when my foot hit some object in the ground. These poles really made a huge difference, and gave me much more confidence in my ability to succeed. I also decided to take a different tent. This tent was easier to put up and get taught. It would be much easier for my arm to deal with.

By the time October came around I was ready, or as ready as I would ever be. This was the day I had dreamt of for so long, and it was finally here.

I had written (when I say written I mean I dictated into my laptop) a small page on my website in regards to the buildup of this adventure. Here is what I wrote:

I am finally able to report a planned hike!! After so long with nothing to report, things are moving so fast I can hardly keep up with them.

My Brother-in-law, Cesar, and I are finally heading off to northern

California to hike the Lost Coast trail. I am nearly a whole year behind schedule, and I attribute this to overreaching when I first posted it last year.

On October 6th 2008 we are flying out to Oakland airport, and from there we are renting a car and driving the 5 or so hours up to Shelter Cove in Northern California. Due to my eyesight, I am still unable to drive so Cesar is handling all of the driving responsibilities.

We will stay overnight in Ukia, which is a small town only a couple of hours from Shelter Cove. On October 7th we will leave the car in the Black Sands car park at Shelter Cove and take the shuttle service up to Mattole Beach, which is the northern part of the Lost Coast Trail and our starting point.

The Lost Coast is situated in the Kings Range National Park in Northern California and is frequently referred to as the wettest part of the US. The wet season begins ironically in October so we should be able to test our waterproof gear to the maximum!

The main reason why we chose this particular time to go is that there is a good chance that we will see some hump backed whales out in the Pacific Ocean. These magnificent creatures are a joy to behold and I hope to take several good photographs if I get a chance.

Although the trail is flat at sea level, the majority of it is on the beach. It is very rocky and difficult to walk on. My leg is still not sufficiently recovered for me to do this without mishap, and I fully expect to spend a large part of the hike flat on my face in the sand!!

Tides are a big problem with this hike, and I do have a tidal chart. Of course, away from a computer I cannot read it so again Cesar is in charge of this vital responsibility.

The other big concern is rogue waves. Several people have been dragged out to sea and drowned by these big, unexpected waves. We need to keep a constant watch out for these.

The Kings Range does have a problem with habituated bears. Whilst these are black bears and not the infamous grizzlies, they are still big and can pose a huge threat to human safety. Hard sided food canisters are mandatory and it is very important to ensure that correct procedures are exercised for the duration of our hike.

Other than rattle snakes, poison ivy and poison oak there are no other major hazards that I am aware of on this trail!!

Most people complete this hike in 3 days/2 nights but there is no way I can complete the hike to this schedule. This is why we have given ourselves a whole week to complete it.

I will take loads of photographs and post them onto my website when I return, and also a full trail diary of how it went.

This is only the start for me. Once I get through this I intend to approach other longer hikes next year. It may take me longer than most other people, but the achievement is well worth the effort.

I gathered my gear and I was ready. I purchased a voice recording device that I could hook up to my laptop. I could then take what I had recorded and convert it into a word document or anything else I desired. I got it so I could maintain a trail diary in California without forgetting anything, which I was very prone to do. It is small, only about 1 inch wide by about 3 inches long, which was perfect for what I was about to do. One more effective method I used to get around my Gerstmanns Syndrome.

Because of my strength and balance issues, it was imperative that I took the lightest gear possible as long as it remained effective in use. Fortunately, I had collected a lot of backpacking gear over the years and I had some of the lightest gear out there. My total pack weight, without food and water was very light at 12lbs. I know some people would think this as heavy, but for the vast majority it is a very lightweight setup. I needed that.

I never knew this until I went to the TLC, but I actually enjoy cooking. More to the point, I think I actually enjoy the fact that I am able to do it on my own. Using my laptop and different colors I am able to prepare just about anything.

Most freeze dried backpacking food is expensive, bulky, and has small portions. After expending energy all day I was always starving when I stopped for dinner. This would be no different. As far as I am aware, the freeze dried food also contains sodium, which I have to avoid nowadays. I pay much closer attention to the food I eat since the stroke, and I try to eat only food that is good for me.

I got a backpacking recipe book and a food dehydrator. I spent an inordinate amount of time scanning the book into my computer (I couldn't find an electronic version) so I could have the directions read out to me. Then I set about making all the food for our trip. Big portions, no sodium, and small packaging. Perfect for our needs.

When the day arrived I was like an excited school child. I didn't know what to expect, but whatever it was, I was ready for it. I knew it was going to be fun, but I didn't think it would be as hilariously funny as it turned out to be. We met some interesting people along the trail who definitely made it entertaining.

CHAPTER 15

I did it! I actually did it! Although I suffered many falls and mishaps along the way, I finally managed to complete the trip that had kept me going through all those dark times in the hospital. All the tears, all the effort, and all the commitment were worth it when I finally completed the Lost Coast Trail. I had climbed my own Mount Everest, and now I was ready for anything. Or so I thought. My world was about to come crashing down once again.

Ever since I had returned home from the TLC things had not been good in my marriage. Alison was going out almost every night she wasn't working, and not coming home until the small hours of the morning. I suspected she was having an affair, but she constantly denied it.

Rightly or wrongly, all my energy and attention was centered on my recovery. Unless someone has been in my position they would never know how difficult it is to recover from such a debilitating injury, and it took all I had to keep my head above the water and keep on swimming against the tide.

I focused not only on the immediate issues of recovery, but also my long term fixed goal of completing the Lost Coast Trail. Everyone needs goals in their lives. In my situation it was imperative that I had something to strive for and to reach for. Without it I firmly believe that I would never have made the recovery that I did. I was hoping that Alison would understand that and work with me as I fought my disabilities.

However, it became clear very early on that Alison either couldn't or wouldn't work with me on this. I think she decided that spending the rest of her life with a disabled stroke survivor was not for her, and she wanted out.

So she began going out all the time. I'm sure it all began when I was away for all that time in the hospitals, and she saw no reason to stop once I got home. She went to the pubs and clubs with her friend and never came home until it was almost daylight. Her dress style became more and more flirtatious, and she stayed out longer and longer.

I confronted her on several occasions, but each time she assured me that everything was fine and that she was just having a good time with her friends. I didn't believe her, but I was too involved with my own recoveries to do anything about it.

Although I was as independent as possible, I still relied on assistance in many areas of my life, and this mainly came from Karen and Phil. Alison had virtually stopped all assistance long ago. My birthday came along, and we had planned to go out to dinner and go to the movies. When the day came she told me that she had changed her plans and was going out with her friends. She never came home until 6am the next morning.

The following Saturday she told me she was working the night shift. As she was a nurse this was normal and I didn't think anything else about it. At least I didn't until Sunday morning when

I was checking our banking online, which is one more benefit of text to speech software. There was an entry from the previous night for the Howard Johnson Hotel, which is located across the road from the night club she had been favoring lately. It was in her name, and it hit me like a sledgehammer.

I immediately confronted her about it, and she stumbled with her words for several minutes while she composed herself. Then she told me that she booked it for her friend as she didn't have a bank account. Her eyes were furtive, and she wouldn't make eye contact with me. Then she grabbed her purse and went shopping for the afternoon.

I was devastated and angry. Had she been lying to me after all? All this time I had been in hospital and trying to recover, had she been having an affair? When she got home I demanded we talk and that this time she had to tell me the truth.

So she did. All of it. She didn't work the previous night. She went to the club with her new boyfriend and spent the night with him. He wasn't the first. There had been several other men in her life before this new one. She had decided that living with me wasn't what she wanted, and couldn't face the future with a disabled man, no matter how much I recovered.

So she had set out to find someone else. She had decided that her latest boyfriend was the one she wanted to have a longer term affair with, and she wanted to end the marriage. I was devastated, angry, upset, betrayed, and completely flattened. I didn't know what to say or do, and I figured it was best if I didn't say anything at that moment because if I did it could get very ugly real fast. So I walked away.

Over the next few days we talked, but she continued going out and then didn't even bother coming home at all so I knew it was pointless. I was hurt to the point of being numb. I was devastated when I realized that while I was spending all that time fighting for my life, my sanity, my independence, and my future, in hospitals and rehabilitation centers, Alison had been running around in clubs and bars with goodness knows who and didn't care one jot if I made it or not.

A duplex had just been made available over the road from our home. I had to stay close to Karen because I needed daily assistance with many different tasks, so this was perfect. Karen and I contacted the owners, paid the deposit and got the keys. Now I was completely on my own.

I still don't know why I did this, but all I took from the house was my reclining chair, my clothes and my camping gear. I left everything else. I had no bed, no pots and pans, no sheets, nothing. And I had no money.

I have a small income from my disability insurance, but nothing that will make it easy for me to survive on. I used all that to pay for the deposit on the duplex. For the next month I relied on the goodwill of friends and family to keep me fed and functioning. It was a time in my life when I really found out who my true friends were, and I have a lot of respect and love for all of them.

Alison quickly moved away from the area which suited me down to the ground. Having the latest boyfriend glaring at me over the road every time I opened my door was not what I wanted so I was glad when they moved.

Phil had some furniture in storage, and between him and our friend Heather that had a truck, they brought it all over and set it up for me. If it wasn't for that, it would have taken me forever to rebuild my basic belongings. At Christmas time friends and family bought me pots, pans, plates and dishes. All the kinds of things that I really needed and greatly appreciated.

At first I needed lots of help as I adjusted to life on my own. Poor Karen and Phil forever had to come over and help me with something or other. But as time moved on I became more and more independent, needing help with only transportation, and anything to do with the public as I was still avoiding any interaction with them that demonstrated my disabilities.

I continued working on my leg and arm, and I was getting stronger and stronger. I still had massive problems with steps, more going down than up. Going up I could grab onto the rail and use my good leg to pull my bad one behind it. Going down, I still grabbed the rail but there is always a point when my left leg was bearing at least some weight and my knee has to bend. That is where I have the greatest issues. I fall over. It is not only painful, but also embarrassing when leaving a packed movie theatre and everyone is staring and laughing at me.

CHAPTER 16

Karen's house had a small duplex built onto the side of it and they shared the same driveway. In February 2010 the duplex became available. As I had completed my six month contract and was now on a month to month contract in my duplex, I decided to move.

The new duplex was larger, in better shape, and cheaper. It was also right next door to Karen and Ben so it was better all around. Money was very tight as always, but we came up with the deposit and once again asked all my wonderful friends for help moving all my belongings (which were not really all that much in all honesty).

I was now divorced, and had settled into my new life pretty well. I had not given up on romance, but I had a very low opinion of myself in that regard. Who would want a middle aged disabled man who can't read or write, and who couldn't drive? I didn't think that anyone would ever want me again, especially for a long term relationship. And who could blame them? Certainly not me.

I had reached a plateau once again with my physical recovery and I wanted to try something different. So I bought a bicycle. I thought it might also help with basic grocery shopping to save Karen from always having to take me.

I thought I was doing well for the first few days. Just like the recumbent bikes in the TLC, my good leg dragged my bad leg around with it, and I was enjoying my new found freedom. My new bike didn't have pedals; it had clips where cycling shoes clipped into them. I had never had this before, and it took me a while to get used to it. I kept forgetting, and when I stopped and tried to lower my leg to the floor for an anchor I would suddenly remember it was clipped into the pedals. By the time I reacted it was too late, and I ended up laying on the ground feeling like a fool. But to me it was freedom.

Everything was going well until April 13th, 2010. Up until this time I had ridden my bike around the local area, both to get used to the bike and to get fitter. On this day I decided I wanted to go further, which was a huge mistake. In fact, it was such a disaster I wrote about it on my website blog. I wrote in a humorous, self-depreciating, slightly exaggerated style, as my nightmare bike ride warranted such a presentation. Here is what I wrote:

How NOT to go on a bike ride!!

I purchased a new (well, at least new to me) bicycle a few weeks ago. Unable to drive for medical reasons, I was slowly going insane staying at home all the time.

Buying a bike was the best of both worlds for me – it gets me out of the house and away from these four walls and also gets me fit and active at the same time. A perfect combination.

For the first few days I rode it around my neighborhood as I hadn't ridden a bike in years and had to get used to it again. This morning, with a lot of stuff weighing heavily on my mind, I decided to be a little more adventurous and go a little further while staying away from the busy roads and all the construction that is happening in Lubbock right now. That was my second mistake today. The first was getting out of bed.

I had planned a route that was about 10 miles and would take me about an hour. As I rode out into the countryside I had a million thoughts of the past few years racing through my mind and missed my turning. It was several miles later that I realized my error. Being stubborn and stupid, I decided to rely on my own warped sense of direction to get me off the farm roads and back into civilization.

So there I am about 2 hours later still riding down these backwater roads thinking that my day just couldn't get any worse. What a crock that was!! The next thing I knew this big old dog appeared out of nowhere and decided that I looked like meals on wheels. Still not used to these cycle clips, I couldn't get my foot out of the clip and this huge hound, foaming at the mouth and looking like the Hound Of The Baskervilles jumped at me, bit my foot and knocked me straight off my bike onto the concrete.

With my arm cut open, Baskerville chomping on my foot and my bike lay on top of me I finally got my foot off the pedal clip. Now as anyone that has ever been in this situation will testify, being lost, tired, and having Baskerville chewing on one's foot does not make for a pleasant day out. So I got up and, making myself as big as possible, I confronted Baskerville with the foot he had been so eagerly chewing on for the last 30 minutes.

Feeling victorious with Baskerville backing right off - at least 2 centimeters - and showing me his pearly whites, I did my best impression of a Lee Van Cleefe stare and got back on my bike. I think the hound from hell had learned his lesson because he didn't follow me. Next time I ride down that road (wherever that road is) I'm taking my bear spray with me…

Having thought that my day had hit rock bottom I immediately found out that it was only just beginning. The wind had picked up and for every foot I gained it seemed like I was pedaling 20 feet backwards. I swear that the stop sign 100 yards ahead was getting further away and it took me about an hour to get there.

I reached the junction and decided to take a break from my traumas and finally use some of the intelligence that I'm supposed to have somewhere tucked away in that brain of mine. I had my Blackberry phone with me and I have a subscription to turn by turn GPS. Now I can get home I thought.

Wrong. I turned it on and all I got was an error message. I have no idea what it said because I can't read, but I didn't need to be able to read to know that it wasn't going to work. It was as though the phone was sending me a huge big finger to look at, and I knew what that meant!!

So picture the scenario. I'm totally lost out in the boondocks, my GPS wasn't working, the wind was roaring at 100MPH in the opposite direction from where I was trying to ride, and I was bleeding from my fight with Megatron. To say that I was somewhat agitated is the understatement of the year.

I decided to keep going down these farm roads until either it got dark and I would rest up in Blair Witch Forest for the night or I would eventually find a road I knew out of there. My cell phone had no signal which probably explains the big finger on the GPS system, and even if it did I couldn't call for help because I had no idea where I was.

Imagine the phone call "Hey, I'm lost, tired, bleeding and need a ride home." "Sure, where are you?" "Err, I don't know". Yeah, that was a great idea.

So there I am cycling down this never ending road thinking I am about to hit Los Angeles when this huge gust of wind hits me from a ridiculous angle. My glasses flew from my head about 100 feet, over a fence and into a field. Great. I stopped, got off the bike and *went to look for them.*

Now, I have major problems climbing up and down stairs as my left leg still has pretty bad issues when I try to raise or lower it. The good thing about cycling is that my good leg can drag my bad leg around with it.

So here I am trying to climb up and over Mt. Everest. Of course I didn't make it and fell splat into a thorn bush (or some other prickly nasty thing) on the other side, scratching and cutting my leg in the process. I spent like an hour searching for my glasses to no avail and eventually gave up.

I still had to negotiate the fence again and sure enough I didn't make it this time either. I fell head first into the only thorn bush in a 100 mile radius this side of the fence, and by this time I was really having a great day.

I got back on my bike and then quickly realized why I can't drive and have to wear glasses. I am completely blind in my left eye and only half sighted in my right. And that is with glasses. Without them I'm like Mr. Magoo in a snow storm and I could hardly see more than a few feet in front of me.

I got back on my bike thankful that the roads were empty (I think I was the only person in the entire world that knew of this road's existence). About three days later I finally rode into Shallowater. How I got there I will never know but somehow I managed it.

I found a burger bar and sat outside eating this 5lb slab of meat wishing it was Baskerville while I waited for Karen, to come and get me. It felt like I had ridden about 130 miles into the strong winds, and I was whacked. I'm nowhere near fit enough for rides of that magnitude. I don't think I have ever been so happy to see Karen in my entire life!!

I'm now having a few days off...

I think it's fairly obvious at this point that I wasn't cut out for bicycles! I did ride it again a few times after that, but not very often. I ended up selling it to a young man who would do it much more justice than I ever could.

CHAPTER 17

Up until this point, my life had been an eclectic mix of humor and tears, victory and defeat, and highs and lows. It was all about to change, and the name of that change was Glenda Lattimore.

As I stated earlier, I had all but given up with romance. I had long since gotten over Alison, but I didn't think anyone would ever see me as a suitable partner ever again. I figured that there were plenty of choices out there for women my age, so why would anyone choose someone who was damaged and had little, if anything to offer?

I was spending the early months of 2010 trying to get stronger and fitter in order to attempt the Colorado Trail later that year in July. I was making my own dehydrated food that I was going to forward to post offices along the route, and I was determined to complete this 500 mile trail, not just for myself, but for all disabled people. I wanted to inspire hope and achievement for all of us, not just the able bodied hikers and athletes that attempt this trail each year. As events unfolded, I didn't attempt the trail this time. Instead, I concentrated on my own personal life, and the wonderful moments that followed. I haven't given up on this majestic trail, and one day I will complete all 500 miles of it.

On March 5th 2010, I joined the online dating world of Match.com. Even though I kept telling myself that I had given up with romance, deep in my heart I knew that I desired a lifetime partner more than anything else in my life. I wanted someone that would see me for who I was, not for what I wasn't or what I couldn't do. I just didn't think that there was anyone out there that would do that. I was wrong.

I looked down the list of ladies around my age that had posted, and my eyes stopped at a picture of a very attractive lady with the most beautiful eyes I had ever seen. I copied her profile into Microsoft Word to make it easier for my programs to read it to me, and I liked what I heard.

Glenda was a nurse who specialized in NICU care for newborn infants, and there was something about her profile that I liked. So I sent a small email to her, briefly stating that I liked her profile and that if she liked mine to get back to me.

I had placed a photograph on the site, and written a small article about myself. I did leave out the fact that I was a stroke survivor and that I had disabilities because I felt nobody would ever respond to that. I wanted to at least have the chance to get to know someone before they ditched me for my disabilities.

It was always my intention to be upfront about my situation, as I owed everyone who ever entered my life, in any kind of capacity, the right to know about my disabilities. But especially someone who was looking to go on a date with me.

I didn't have high expectations of getting any kind of reply, so I was surprised when, a few days later, I did. We communicated via email for a few days, then by telephone, and eventually agreed to meet up for dinner.

We met at the local Cracker Barrel, and I thoroughly enjoyed our first meeting. I greatly appreciated her warm personality, and she had a wonderful sense of humor. One more thing that I really liked was that she was very intelligent and loved history, which is one of my biggest interests in life. It also helped that she was the most beautiful lady I had ever seen in my entire life. It was at this meeting that I came clean with her about my life. I liked her, and if we were to meet again, I wanted her to know everything before she made that decision.

I didn't expect I would ever hear from her again, so I was pleasantly surprised to get a call from her the next day. We agreed to meet again, this time at a steak restaurant. I was over the moon, and looked forward eagerly to meeting with her again.

Our second dinner was just as wonderful as the first. I really enjoyed our conversations, and the time just flew by. We seemed to have a lot of things in common, and we had plenty to talk about. When we parted we arranged to speak the next day, and by now I was quietly optimistic that I may have found someone. I liked everything I had heard and seen so far, and I wanted to get to know her better.

The next day came and went and I didn't hear from her. She wasn't answering her calls either. I didn't want to bother her, so I only called a couple of times. I didn't want to be a stalker!! A couple of days went by and I thought she had decided not to see me anymore, which is what I had always expected from the start. I was shocked, therefore, when I finally did get a call from her around three days later. I was even more shocked when she explained what had happened.

The evening after our dinner she had started being sick, and it had just gotten worse and worse. She was eventually taken into hospital and treated for chronic food poisoning and dehydration. No wonder she didn't call me! Typical, I thought, I finally meet someone I like and all I do is give her food poisoning – and I didn't even cook it!! I felt responsible as I suggested that we eat at that particular establishment, and I felt terribly guilty.

Thankfully she made a swift recovery, but I thought there was no way she would ever eat dinner with me again. Sure enough, several weeks went by and I hadn't heard from her, and I didn't call after the first day or so because I was terrified of being labeled a stalker, so I assumed she had, quite understandably, moved on.

One evening I came home from Karen's around 10pm and I noticed a missed call on my phone that I had left behind. Nobody ever really called me in the evenings, and I was more shocked to see it was Glenda that had called. I called back immediately, and we talked for ages, laughing at the mishap in the restaurant.

From that moment on we saw each other all the time. The more I learned about her the more I liked her, and the more I liked her, the more I wanted to know about her. Her sense of humor is a perfect fit for mine, and her personality and intellect are a perfect match. We have so many similar interests that we could talk for days on end and never get tired of it. She completely overlooked my disabilities and saw me for the person I am, not for what I used to be, or what I could be, and that means everything to me.

I was falling head over heels in love with her, and in October 2010 we went on a cruise together to Jamaica, Grand Caymans, and Cozumel. True to form, this turned out to be a disaster of a cruise. We sailed into a tropical storm, and when we pulled into Montego Bay, we waved at Jamaica as we sailed out again. They wouldn't allow us to dock as it was too stormy. The next morning we pulled into the Grand Caymans. I waved at it as we immediately left again. As yesterday, it was too rough to dock. We finally did manage to get off the boat in Cozumel, and it was a great relief to finally get onto dry land. The next day the cruise ended as we went back to Galveston Island.

While we were in Galveston, we stopped at the TLC. It was the first time I had been back there since I left, and it was in fact the first time that I had ever walked in, out, or around it. I was completely wheelchair bound all the time I was there, so that made the visit even more emotional than it already was.

I made a point of visiting Dr. Z. Dennis, in fact all the staff, remembered me as soon as I walked in and opened my mouth. I put it down to my distinct British accent, but they assured me that it was because I was one of the few patients they see with Gerstmanns Syndrome and because of my positive, light hearted attitude when I was there. That made me feel good. Dr. Z told me that he had written a thesis study on my story; such was the level of interest I generated when I was down there. They were all amazed at how well I had recovered, and wished me well for the future.

The visit to the TLC had been more emotional than I ever imagined it was going to be. It brought back everything to me, even as far as the voices and the facial expressions of my fellow patients as we struggled with our life changing disabilities together. It was a spiritual cleansing for me, and it had a much deeper meaning than I had ever envisaged. I was very glad we went.

On September 13th 2008, Galveston Island was hit by hurricane Ike. The whole island suffered terrible damage, and the human tragedies were devastating, especially coming so soon after hurricane Katrina. Although the TLC is located several blocks from the sea front, it was devastated. There are markings on the outside of the gymnasium wall that indicate how high the water levels rose on that fateful day. If I had been sat in my wheelchair at that point, I would have been several feet under water, and the damage was extensive. All the patients and staff had been relocated inland, and thankfully no-one was injured. They were still in the process of rebuilding the TLC when we visited such was the devastation caused by hurricane Ike.

CHAPTER 18

On October 3rd, 2010, Glenda and I were on the ship enjoying our cruise. By this time I was hopelessly in love with her, and I knew I wanted to spend the rest of my life with her. She is the most wonderful human being I have ever met, and I was blessed and honored to have her in my life.

I had purchased a ring that I knew she liked, and I got down on my knees in our room and asked her to marry me. My heart was pounding, and I was as nervous as I had ever been in my entire life. I truthfully didn't know what she was going to say, but she just looked at me, smiled, and said "Yes, I will marry you". My heart melted, and I felt deep waves of emotion and love sweep over my entire body. I was the happiest man in the world. We became engaged on that day.

Shortly after we returned home after the cruise, we moved in together, and on May 17th 2011 we were married in a small, beautiful church in Lubbock, Texas. It was the happiest day of my life, and everything went perfectly.

Soon after, we moved into our new home, and we continue to be very happy as we share our lives together.

In the space of five years I have gone from the very depths of despair, when I had no hope and no future, from losing everything - physical, emotional, and material, to a future full of promise and happiness, where riches are not measured by how much money we have in the bank, but by the love we have in our hearts, not only for each other and our families, but for our future and the amazing plans that we make together. That for us is true happiness and wealth.

My life is an example of an extreme rollercoaster ride of lows, emotions, setbacks, and life altering injuries, to the highs of finally meeting my soul mate, and recovering from debilitating injuries when I never thought I would walk again. My story is one of eternal hope, and this is why I want to share it with anyone else in the world that is, or has been, or will be, struggling with major issues and cannot see a way out. I am here to testify that there is always hope, and if we never give up, no matter how hard the journey, there is a light at the end of the tunnel. I hope to see you all there one day.

CONCLUSION

Today, I continue fighting every single moment for my recovery. I am able to walk unaided with only a slightly discernible limp that becomes exaggerated when I get tired. My arm and hand work very well, and I am able to grasp most anything I desire and hold doors open with it.

I continue to have major issues with stairs, and I constantly tumble and fall in movie theatres, restaurants; anywhere where there are stairs or steps. I cannot raise my left arm above my head without intervention from others or my own good arm, and I cannot carry anything heavier than a half-gallon of milk without dropping it.

I still cannot read or write. Letters and numbers are nothing but mysterious symbols from a Dan Brown novel. My math skills are almost nonexistent. My 7 year old grandson can read, write and count better than I can. I am blind in my left eye, and my night vision is negligible.

'Some recovery' I hear people saying, and they may be right. However, I don't see it that way. I can walk where I was once paralyzed, I can feed myself and open my own doors where once my arm was in a sling because my arm and shoulder were separating with subluxation. I take my own showers, and see to my own personal hygiene where once I battled for even a modicum of privacy.

I realized a goal that at one time seemed destined to be no more than a dream. I may have stumbled through it, and completed it in record slow time, but I did it. Nothing gave me more pleasure at the time than knowing I had fought against all the odds to be in northern California in October 2008 and hiked the Lost Coast Trail.

I went through the depths of despair when I thought that my wife was behind me all the way in my recovery, only to find out that she couldn't have cared any less if she had tried, and yet, even when I was suffering from all my disabilities and fighting for my own future, I met the lady of my dreams and my soul mate in Glenda. She encourages me, and supports me in my daily battles, and overlooks what I can't do in favor of the many things that I can do. This is true love, and I am the most fortunate man in the world to be experiencing it at this time of my life. I absolutely adore Glenda, and I would do anything for her. She is a lady in a million.

I have 2 wonderful children who stood by me every step of the way, and I owe them a debt of gratitude I will never be able to repay. I now have 3 beautiful grandchildren who make it all worthwhile, and now we have an extended family that makes my life complete.

No sir, I have made massive gains in my recovery, and in the process I have learned the meaning of humility, patience, persistence and dedication. If I can do it - a simple middle aged Englishman with absolutely no special skills whatsoever, then anyone can do it. This is the story of how I did it.

Jim Chatterton

ETERNAL HOPE

ABOUT THE AUTHOR

Jim Chatterton originally comes from Derbyshire, England. He moved to America with his family in 1999. He currently lives in Texas with his wife and family.

Made in the USA
San Bernardino, CA
10 April 2013